D1555180

LITTLE RUSSIAN PHILOKALIA

SERIES

LITTLE RUSSIAN PHILOKALIA
I
ST. SERAPHIM OF SAROV

St. Seraphim of Sarov

LITTLE RUSSIAN
PHILOKALIA

VOLUME I

Saint Seraphim of Sarov

Spiritual Instructions
translated by Fr. Seraphim Rose

ST. HERMAN OF ALASKA BROTHERHOOD
2008

Copyright © 2008 by the
St. Herman of Alaska Brotherhood

Address all correspondence to:
St. Herman of Alaska Brotherhood
P.O. Box 70
Platina, California 96076

First Edition, 1978; Second Edition, 1983; Third Edition, 1991; Fourth Edition, 1996; Fifth Edition, 2008.

Front cover: A portrait of St. Seraphim which was widely distributed at the time of his canonization in 1903.
Back cover: Valaam painting of St. Seraphim.

Publishers Cataloging-in-Publication

Serafim, Sarovskii, Saint, 1754–1833.
    [Selections. English. 2008.]
    Spiritual instructions / Saint Seraphim of Sarov ; translated by Fr. Seraphim Rose. — 5th ed. — Platina, Calif. : St. Herman of Alaska Brotherhood, 2008.
    p. ; cm.
    (Little Russian philokalia ; v. 1)
    Includes bibliographical references and index.
    Previous edition: 1996.
    Translated from the Russian.
    ISBN: 978-0-938635-30-7
    1. Spiritual life—Orthodox Eastern Church. 2. Christian life—Orthodox Eastern authors. 3. Orthodox Eastern Church—Doctrines. 4. Serafim, Sarovskii, Saint, 1754–1833. I. Rose, Seraphim, 1934–1982. II. Title.

BX382 .S37 2008
248.4/819—dc22
                                                   90064253

PREFACE
to the *Little Russian Philokalia* Series

THERE have been several attempts to compile a collection of Russian Fathers similar to that of the Greek *Philokalia*, simply because a great multitude of such outstanding teachers existed in Russia. They were worthy Fathers both in the lucidity of their writings and in the purity of their personal lives: St. Nilus of Sora with his "Skete Rule," St. Joseph of Volokolamsk with his "Russian Lausiac History," St. Dorotheus of Youg with his "Spiritual Flowers," and the great Elder Basil of Poiana Marului, just to mention a few who lived before the 19th century. By that time there had been such an increase of truly great ascetic authors that it became inevitable that such a collection should be made. The best collection that was published was called *Elders' Counsels of the 18th and 19th Centuries,* compiled by Bishop Nikodim of Belgorod, a new martyr who was brutally killed in 1918. It was printed in Moscow in 1913 by the Russian monastery on Mt. Athos, St. Panteleimon's, as a companion volume (vol. 15) to the same author's *Russian Ascetics of the 18th and 19th Centuries.* This is how Bishop Nikodim introduces his 600-page volume:

"For the last two centuries there have been many men of holy and God-pleasing life in Holy Russia. These men taught not only by the example of their life, but many of them also by wise counsel. These wise words of instruction in righteous life are already available in part for whoever thirsts to know the right way of life. The writings of the hierarchs Tikhon of Zadonsk, Demetrius of Rostov, Theophan the Recluse, Ignatius Brianchaninov, and others have been published in volumes of their complete works. The instructions of the Optina Elders, of George of Zadonsk, of St. Seraphim of Sarov and many others have also been published either in their biographies or in collections of their letters. But many instructions of others were published either in old magazines or books which have become rarities and are not available now to the general public. Trying to fill in this gap, the monastery (St. Panteleimon's) is offering this volume—a fragment of the Elders' Counsels, and in place of an introduction it offers 'An Outline of Russian Ascetical Literature in the Last Two Centuries' for those who wish to know more, and to find out where to seek this treasure of Russia's wisdom."

Thus, even this volume of 27 Fathers is not complete. Besides the omitted Fathers just listed, there is no mention of such giants as Blessed Paisius Velichkovsky, Elder Basilisk of Siberia, Abbot Nazarius of Valaam, Elder Adrian of Youg, Archimandrite Alexander of Arzamas, the Elders of Sarov, and of course, St. John of Kronstadt.

Another compilation was made by the holy Archbishop Theophan of Poltava (1872–1940), called "The Russian Philokalia," but he arranged his selections by topics, and apparently he did not intend to make a compilation of *all* Russian Fathers. The manuscript of this work was lost during the Second World War, and thus it was never printed, but was highly saluted by Archbishop Averky of Jordanville who knew it in manuscript form.

In the 1930s Valaam Monastery published two volumes, compiled and written by Abbot Chariton of Valaam, with 860 pages in all, of excerpts (mostly from Bishops Theophan and Ignatius), limited to the subject of the Jesus Prayer. The two volumes, entitled *The Mental Art: On the Jesus Prayer* (1936), and *What is the Jesus Prayer according to the Tradition of the Orthodox Church* (1938), are of great value, and they have been called by some a "Russian Philokalia." A partial translation of this work has appeared in English, entitled *The Art of Prayer*, but this volume bears little resemblance to the two volumes in Russian and contains only a quarter of the whole work.

For us, the value of these Russian Fathers lies in the surprising timeliness of their counsel. Their attention is directed to a situation almost contemporary to that in which we ordinary Orthodox Christians find ourselves today.

To make a collection that would be timely was, of course, also the main concern of such great Fathers as both Theophans (the Recluse and the Archbishop of Poltava) who, being themselves in the spirit of the authors of the ancient *Philokalia,* were concerned to help the men and women of their time to come closer to their Fathers. With this in mind, when translating and editing his five-volume *Philokalia* in Russian, Theophan the Recluse somewhat changed the order of the Fathers found both in the Greek and Slavonic editions, and replaced some authors with others. (For example, he devoted a whole volume, the fourth, to St. Theodore the Studite, in order to give a more practical, all-encompassing approach for the monastics of the latter times who might otherwise underemphasize the basic discipline of coenobitic life; for the same reason he also at times omitted or abridged texts.) Such work proved to be quite useful, and we can see now what a flowering of genuine monasticism occurred precisely under his influence. A disregard, such as has recently become noticeable in the West, for Bishop Theophan's invaluable contribution would indeed be unfortunate and near-sighted, for historically one may see that those Orthodox countries that did not possess a teacher of such magnitude did not reap such a spiritual harvest as did Russian Orthodoxy under his (and, of course, others') influence. That part of the Orthodox tradition in the world today which is spiritually still alive is deeply indebted precisely to such teachers as Bishops Theophan and Ignatius and others like them, who are our link with the ancient Fathers and are our beacons for the future.

Therefore it is of no small importance to present the Russian Fathers of recent centuries in an anthology, a *Little Russian Philokalia*, as intermediaries between ourselves and the great Fathers of the Greek *Philokalia*, who at times speak far above the ability of present-day readers to receive and assimilate; these latter writings are directed almost exclusively to monastics of advanced life and total seclusion from the world—that is, only to a very few. Our contemporaries in the English-speaking world, by reading just the Greek *Philokalia* without properly applying it their own condition, might find an opportunity to depart from the narrow path, exalting themselves by dreaming of a state for which they are not prepared. Premature or unprepared reading of the *Philokalia* can alienate one from the daily task of an obedient fulfillment of the basic commandments of God; to those who are thus puffed up, this latter path can even begin to seem bland and unattractive. We must bear in mind that we live in a time of fakery and universal "imitation" in all phases of our modern life. All our outstanding teachers of spiritual life, such as Archbishops Theophan of Poltava, Vitaly and Averky of Jordanville, Andrew of New-Diveyevo, John and Tikhon of San Francisco, Elders Philemon, Barsanuphius and Michael of Valaam—taught us to be aware of our handicapped state and not to soar too high above everyday reality. Sad indeed is the confusion and falling away from the genuine Orthodox mentality of neophytes who do not keep to this instruction. (The Valaam and Optina Elders strictly forbade, for example, the reading of such texts as the "Hymns" of St. Symeon the New Theologian.)

In this respect the humble advice given by the holy men of the *Little Russian Philokalia*—which we will now present, with God's help, in small volumes—may render an inestimable service to a true seeker of salvation, a follower of Christ's narrow path of unceasing toil and humility. For this, after all, *is* the original and basic purpose of the *Philokalia*.

May these little volumes aid the English-speaking world in walking on the way that is known as the Royal Path.

Hieromonk Herman
St. Herman of Alaska Monastery
October 14, 1979
Nameday of Elder Nazarius of Valaam

CONTENTS

Lithograph showing scenes of the life and miracles of St. Seraphim, 1903.

INTRODUCTION

The Life of Saint Seraphim

THE BEST KNOWN of the Orthodox saints of modern times, St. Seraphim of Sarov, has much to teach the Orthodox Christians of these last times. Unfortunately, the striking nature of some of his spiritual experiences—which indeed stand in glaring contrast to the ordinary Christian experience of our days—has led some to miss the whole point of his teaching. Some are so dazzled by his visions and his all-embracing love that they try to follow him into the most exalted spheres of spiritual life without even the most elementary foundation in Orthodox knowledge and practice; others try artificially to set his "spirituality" against the "institutionalized Church," as if the two could be separated; still others would make him to be a "charismatic" figure who justifies the empty ecumenical "spirituality" of our own poor days; and a few imagine him to be a "guru" whose experience places him "beyond Christianity" and all religious traditions.

All such interpretations—which only bring spiritual harm and disaster to those who follow them—fail to understand St. Seraphim in the context of the religious tradition that produced him as one of its greatest flowerings: Orthodox Christianity in 18th-century Russia.

St. Seraphim (his worldly name was Prochor Moshnin) was born in 1754 in Kursk, in the heart of Holy Russia, to a pious merchant family. Raised in the fear of God and strict Orthodox life, he also knew very early the mercies of God at first hand; at the age of ten he was miraculously healed of a serious affliction by the Mother of God through her Kursk Icon (which is now in America and continues to work miracles).

Once he learned to read, the boy Prochor immersed himself in the spiritual world of basic Christian literature: the Scriptures, the Horologion (containing the daily cycle of church services), the Psalter, and the *Lives of Saints*. He spent all the time he could in church (where services would go on for many hours every day), and thought only of God and the spiritual world. A deep desire for spiritual things being thus kindled in him, he began to long to serve God in the monastic calling. At the age of 19, on a pilgrimage to the holy places of Kiev, he received the counsel of the holy recluse Dositheus (actually a woman) to "go to Sarov"; and after a short time this is what he did—spending the rest of his life in this remarkable Monastery.

The Hermitage of Sarov had been founded early in the 18th century by the Elder John. The first settlers here were cave dwellers, and the Monastery always remained a place of severe ascetic life, at the same time handing down the ancient monastic tradition of inward spiritual activity, the mental prayer of Jesus. Eighteenth-century Russia, although it was a time of monastic decline when compared with the flowering of the 14th to the 17th centuries, still had a number of fathers (and mothers) who kept alive the ancient tradition of Christian spirituality. The great monastic revival inspired by the great Elder Paisius Velichkovsky and his disciples at the end of the 18th century produced such remarkable spiritual fruits (notably the clairvoyant Elders of Optina Monastery) precisely because the Russian soil had been prepared beforehand by an unbroken tradition of monastic struggle and spiritual life.

Blessed Paisius translated the patristic texts on spiritual life, most notably the anthology known as the *Philokalia*. St. Seraphim made use of this book, which he probably received from Elder Nazarius of Sarov, one of the spiritual elders who prepared its publication; but the *Philokalia* was published in 1794, and St. Seraphim was spiritually formed before this, having read numerous other patristic books that taught the same spiritual doctrine. There is nothing whatever that is "new" in the spiritual face of St. Seraphim; all is from the Holy Fathers, of whom he is a most faithful disciple, appearing in the latter times like some great desert Father of antiquity, like a new St. Macarius the Great.

In Sarov, St. Seraphim went through the standard monastic period of trial: he was placed in obedience to a spiritual father and was tested at various labors in the bread and prosphora bakeries, the carpenter shop, at chopping wood, as candlelighter. Church services were long, as was his cell rule of prayer. In addition to the difficult monastic discipline, he was severely ill for three years—a trial he bore with humility and trust in God—until being healed by a vision of the Mother of God.

At the age of 27 St. Seraphim was tonsured a monk, and a few months later was ordained deacon. He served as deacon for nearly seven years, entering deeply into the meaning of the Church's services. Often he saw angels; and once, on Great Thursday, as he stood before the Royal Doors in the middle of the Liturgy, he saw Christ Himself in the air surrounded by angels. Unable to continue serving, he was conducted away and stood for several hours in ecstasy.

At the age of 34 he was ordained priest, and the next year his elder, Abbot Pachomius, on his deathbed entrusted to St. Seraphim the spiritual guidance of the sisters of the nearby Diveyevo Convent—a task he fulfilled so well that even today, fifty years after it was destroyed, it is still remembered as "St. Seraphim's Diveyevo." Just at this time he also received the blessing of the new Abbot to begin life as a hermit in the forest around Sarov. Here in a small cabin he performed a long rule of prayer, labored much, and read the Scriptures and Holy Fathers. On Sundays he would come to the Monastery to attend the Liturgy and receive Holy Communion, returning to the forest with his supply of bread for the week. For one period of three years he ate nothing but a certain herb called "sneet."

In 1804 the saint was attacked by robbers and beaten almost to death. The Mother of God appeared to him in his affliction, together with the Apostles Peter and John the Theologian, saying of him: "This is one of our kind." After this attack he was bent over and walked always with a staff.

Now the saint undertook yet greater struggles. Returning to his forest desert, he undertook an exploit like that of the ancient pillar saints of Syria: for a thousand days and nights he spent the better part of his time kneeling on a stone not far from his cell, constantly calling out to God with the prayer of the publican: "O God, be merciful to me a sinner." Strengthened by divine grace for this humanly impossible task, he entered into open battle with the demons at this time, like St. Anthony of old in the tombs; often he would see the demons, whom he would only describe as "foul."

In 1807, his last elder and instructor, Abbot Isaiah, died; and the saint went into absolute seclusion, refusing to see anyone and maintaining an absolute silence for three years. He no longer came to the Monastery even for Divine Services on Sunday, enduring with patience the great cross of total isolation and silence, by which he yet more crucified the passions and lusts of the old man.

Some of the inexperienced brethren of the Monastery, however, became scandalized that the saint did not seem to be receiving Holy Communion; and the Monastery elders requested him to return (1810). In his monastery cell he remained in silence and seclusion, continuing just as in his forest cell to read the whole daily cycle of services, except for the Liturgy, saying the prayer of Jesus, and especially reading the New Testament (which he went through once a week). During this time he was granted visions of heavenly mysteries, beholding the mansions of heaven with many of the saints.

After five years of this seclusion within the Monastery, St. Seraphim, by a special revelation, opened the door of his cell for all who desired to see him; but still he continued his spiritual exercises without paying any attention to his visitors or answering their questions. After five more years the Mother of God again appeared to him, together with Sts. Onuphrius the Great and Peter of Mt. Athos, instructing him to end his silence and speak for the benefit of others. Now he greeted all who came with a prostration, a kiss and the Paschal greeting: "Christ is risen!" Everyone he called "my joy." In 1825, the Mother of God again appeared to him and blessed him to return to his forest cell.

For the last eight years of his life St. Seraphim lived in the forest of Sarov and received the thousands of pilgrims who came to him to ask his prayers and spiritual counsel. The saint now was manifest as a clairvoyant wonderworker, a grace-filled vessel of the action of the Holy Spirit. No one—monk, layman, or nun (whether of Diveyevo or of the several other convents which arose with his blessing)—left him without consolation and an answer to their spiritual need. He was in constant contact with the world above; twelve times in all, the Mother of God Herself appeared to him. He died kneeling before an icon of the Mother of God of "Tender Feeling" on January 2, 1833.

INTRODUCTION

Having led a heavenly life on earth, like the great desert saints of antiquity, even in these latter times of spiritual desolation, St. Seraphim is an instructor and an inspirer of the true Christian life. His Spiritual Instructions—like his celebrated Conversation with Motovilov on the Acquisition of the Holy Spirit—contain no new teaching, but simply repeat in modern times the age-old Christian teaching of the great Fathers whom he constantly cites: Sts. Basil the Great, Gregory the Theologian, John Chrysostom, Macarius the Great, Dionysius the Areopagite, Ambrose of Milan, Isaac the Syrian, Symeon the New Theologian, the Fathers of the *Philokalia.* These, with the Holy Scriptures, the *Lives of Saints,* and the Church services—all in the context of the living Sarov tradition of spiritual life—are his sources, and he is a faithful transmitter of their teaching: fear of God; heedfulness to oneself; not trusting the impulses of one's own heart but becoming so immersed in God's word that one learns to "swim in the law of the Lord"; working out one's salvation with patience, humility, repentance, forgiveness; acquiring the Spirit of peace, the Holy Spirit, which is the end of all our spiritual labors; placing first God and His love, which kindles our cold hearts and inspires us to follow Him, to know and to love Him. This teaching is not complex; but in our own days, when the love of many has grown cold and the salt is going out of Christianity, it is almost impossible to follow. Only with great humility on our part—which we can learn from the profound humility of "poor Seraphim," as he called himself—can we hope to receive and apply this teaching of the true Christian spiritual life to our own poor Christian lives.

By the prayers of our holy Father Seraphim, may we understand his words and practice them, according to our strength, for the salvation of our souls!

Hieromonk Seraphim (Rose)
Nativity, 1978

Portrait of St. Seraphim, 1832. This portrait was painted during his lifetime and is preserved today in the New Diveyevo Convent, Spring Valley, New York.

I

Spiritual Instructions

St. Seraphim praying on the rock.
An old lithograph from Diveyevo Convent.

The Spiritual Instructions

to Laymen and Monks

of Our Father Among the Saints

Saint Seraphim of Sarov

THE SPIRITUAL INSTRUCTIONS of the great saint of Sarov Monastery are here presented for the first time in the English language, as translated from L. Denisov's *Life* (Moscow, 1904). This important work appears in its entirety: 43 sections, following the order of the original edition.

In 1837 the first biography of St. Seraphim was compiled by Hieromonk Sergius of St. Sergius Holy Trinity Lavra near Moscow, whose abbot at that time was a spiritual son of the saint, Archimandrite Anthony. The *Instructions* were a supplement to this *Life*, being the teaching of St. Seraphim as compiled from conversations with him; the saint himself put nothing of his teaching into writing. Fr. Anthony took an active part in the compilation of this book, and he subsequently presented it for approval to Metropolitan Philaret of Moscow, who had great reverence for the saint.

Having thoroughly examined the manuscript, Metropolitan Philaret returned it to Fr. Anthony and in an accompanying letter wrote: *I am returning to you the exhortations or* Spiritual Instructions *of Fr. Seraphim, which I have examined. I have allowed myself the liberty of changing or completing certain expressions, partly to improve the language, partly so that the thought, at times incomplete and unusually expressed, would not give rise to misinterpretation or controversy. Examine these and let me know if I have changed or harmed anything in the thoughts of the Starets.*

Portrait-icon of St. Seraphim from Diveyevo Convent;
from the end of the 19th or the beginning of the 20th century.

Thanks to the personal intercession in the reluctant Synod of this out-standing hierarch, the book was published and veneration of St. Seraphim took the right course, the saint (canonized in 1903) becoming a major inspiration to Orthodox Russians for a century and more thereafter. May the publication of these *Instructions* in English now inspire Orthodox Americans as well!

I.

GOD

GOD IS A FIRE that warms and kindles the heart and inward parts. And so, if we feel in our hearts coldness, which is from the devil—for the devil is cold—then let us call upon the Lord, and He will come and warm our hearts with perfect love not only for Him, but for our neighbor as well. And from the presence of warmth the coldness of the hater of good will be driven away.

The Fathers wrote, when they were asked: Seek the Lord, but do not be curious as to His dwelling place.

Where God is, there is no evil. Everything that comes from God brings peace and profit and leads a man to humility and self-condemnation.

God shows us His love for mankind not only when we do good, but also when we offend and displease Him. How patiently He endures our transgressions; and when He chastises, how mercifully He chastises!

Do not call God just, says St. Isaac; for His justice is not evident in your deeds. If David called Him just and righteous, His Son, on the other hand, showed us that He is rather good and merciful. Where is His justice? We were sinners, and Christ died for us. (St. Isaac the Syrian, Homily 90.)

A man becomes perfect in the sight of God to the extent that he follows in His footsteps; in the true age God will reveal His face to him. For the righteous, to the degree that they enter into contemplation of Him, behold His image as in a mirror; but there they will behold the revelation of Truth.

If you do not know God, it is impossible for love of Him to be awakened in you; and you cannot love God if you do not see Him. The vision of God comes from knowledge of Him; for contemplation of Him does not precede knowledge of Him.

One should not think about the doings of God when one's stomach is full; on a full stomach there can be no vision of the Divine mysteries.

2.

THE MYSTERY OF THE HOLY TRINITY

IN ORDER to look upon the Most Holy Trinity one must ask the aid of those who taught about the Trinity—St. Basil the Great, St. Gregory the Theologian, and St. John Chrysostom—whose intercession is able to draw upon men the blessing of the Most Holy Trinity. But one should be warned not to attempt to look directly for oneself.

3.

THE REASONS WHY JESUS CHRIST
CAME INTO THE WORLD

THE REASONS WHY Jesus Christ, the Son of God, came into the world are these:

1. The love of God for the human race: *For God so loved the world that He gave His only begotten Son* (John 3:16).

2. The restoration in fallen humanity of the image and likeness of God, as the holy Church celebrates it: *Man who, being made in the image of God, had become corrupt through sin, and was full of vileness, and had fallen away from the better life Divine, doth the wise Creator restore anew* (first Canon of the Matins for the Nativity of Christ, ode 1).

3. The salvation of men's souls: *For God sent not His Son into the world to condemn the world, but that the world through Him might be saved* (John 3:17).

And so we, in conformance with the purposes of our Redeemer, the Lord Jesus Christ, should spend our life in accordance with this Divine teaching, so that through it we may obtain the salvation of our souls.

4.

FAITH

BEFORE ANYTHING ELSE one must believe in God, *that He is, and that He is a rewarder of them that diligently seek Him* (Heb. 11:6).

Faith, according to the teaching of St. Antioch, is the beginning of our union with God. One who truly believes is a stone in the temple of God; he is prepared for the edifice of God the Father, raised to the heights by the power of Jesus Christ, that is, of the Cross, with the aid of ropes, that is, the grace of the Holy Spirit.

Faith without works is dead (James 2:26), and the works of faith are: love, peace, long-suffering, mercy, humility, rest from all works (as God Himself rested from His works), bearing of the Cross, and life in the Spirit. Only such faith can be considered true. True faith cannot be without works; one who truly believes will unfailingly have works as well.

5.

HOPE

ALL WHO HAVE FIRM HOPE in God are raised up to Him and enlightened by the radiance of the eternal Light.

If a man has no care whatever for himself because of love for God and virtuous deeds, knowing that God will take care of him—such hope is true and wise. But if a man takes care for his own affairs and turns with prayer to God only when unavoidable misfortunes overtake him and he sees no way of averting them by his own power, only then beginning to hope in God's aid—such hope is vain and false. True hope seeks the Kingdom of God alone and is convinced that everything earthly that is necessary for this transitory life will unfailingly be given.

The heart cannot have peace until it acquires this hope. It gives peace to the heart and brings joy into it. Concerning this hope the most venerable and holy lips of the Savior have said: *Come unto Me, all ye that labor and are heavy laden, and I will give you rest* (Matt. 11:28); that is, have hope in Me, and you will have relief from labor and fear.

In the Gospel of St. Luke it is said of Symeon: *And it was revealed unto him by the Holy Spirit, that he should not see death, before he had seen the Lord's Christ* (Luke 2:26). And he did not kill his hope, but awaited the desired Savior of the world and, joyfully taking Him into his arms, said: Lord, now lettest Thou Thy servant depart into Thy Kingdom, which I have desired, for I have obtained my hope—Christ the Lord.

6.

LOVE OF GOD

HE WHO HAS attained perfect love exists in this life as if he did not exist. For he considers himself a stranger to the visible, patiently awaiting the invisible. He has been completely changed into love of God and has forgotten every other love.

He who loves himself cannot love God. But he who, for love of God, does not love himself, loves God.

He who truly loves God considers himself a pilgrim and a stranger on this earth; for in his yearning toward God with soul and mind, he contemplates Him alone.

The soul that is filled with love of God, at the time of its departure from the body, does not fear the prince of the air, but takes flight with the angels as if from a foreign country to its native land.

7.

THE FEAR OF GOD

A MAN WHO HAS TAKEN upon himself to travel the path of internal mindfulness must have above all the fear of God, which is the beginning of wisdom.

Upon his mind there must always be engraved these words of the prophet: *Serve the Lord with fear, and rejoice with trembling* (Ps. 2:11).

He should travel this path with the utmost care and with reverence for everything holy, and not negligently.

Otherwise, he must take heed lest there should apply to him the Divine decree: *Cursed be he that doeth the work of the Lord negligently* (Jer. 48:10).

Reverent carefulness is necessary here because this sea—that is, the heart, with its thoughts and desires, which one must cleanse by means of mindfulness—is great and vast, *and there are numberless reptiles there* (Ps. 103:27), that is, numerous vain, unjust, and impure thoughts generated by evil spirits.

8.

THE KEEPING OF RECOGNIZED TRUTHS

ONE SHOULD NOT OPEN ONE'S HEART to another without need; out of a thousand you may find only one who would keep your secret. When we do not keep it to ourselves, how can we hope that another could keep it?

With a worldly man one should speak of human matters; but with a man who possesses a spiritual intelligence one should speak of heavenly matters.

People who are filled with spiritual wisdom judge concerning the spirit of a given person according to the Holy Scriptures, looking to see whether his words conform to the will of God; and from this they draw their conclusions about him.

When you happen to be among people in the world, you should not speak about spiritual matters, especially when no desire to listen can be noticed in them. In such a case one should follow the teaching of St. Dionysius the Areopagite (in *The Celestial Hierarchies,* Ch. 2): "Having yourself become divine through knowledge of divine things, and having concealed holy truths as one whole in the depths of your soul, carefully guard them from the uninitiated; for as the Scripture says, one should not throw before swine the pure, bright, and precious adornment of mental pearls." One must keep in mind the word of the Lord: *Neither cast ye your pearls before swine, lest they trample them under their feet, and turn again and rend you* (Matt. 7:6).

And therefore you should strive by every means to keep to yourself the treasure of your spiritual gifts. Otherwise you will lose it, and not find it again. For, according to the tested teaching of St. Isaac the Syrian, better the help that comes from watchfulness than the help that comes from experience (Homily 89).

When need arises, or the situation calls for it, then you should act openly to the glory of God, according to the saying: *Them that honor Me I will honor* (I Kings 2:30), because then the way has already been opened.

9.

LOQUACITY

B Y ITSELF LOQUACITY with those whose temperaments are opposed to our own is enough to disrupt the interior balance of a mindful person.

But most lamentable of all is the fact that because of this the fire which our Lord Jesus Christ came to light upon the earth of human hearts can be extinguished. For "nothing so cools the fire that a monk draws from the Holy Spirit into his heart for the sanctification of his soul, as much as communication and loquacity and any conversation, except for conversation with children concerning God's mysteries, which aids their growth in knowledge of God and contact with Him" (St. Isaac the Syrian, Homily 8).

One should especially keep oneself away from the society of the feminine sex; for just as a wax candle, even though unlit, will melt when placed amongst burning candles, so the heart of a monk will imperceptibly weaken from conversation with women. Concerning this St. Isidore of Pelusium explains thus: "If there are some conversations that corrupt good habits, then they are the ones that are conducted with women, even if these be quite decent, because they can secretly corrupt the inward man by means of bad thoughts; and even though the body be clean, the soul nevertheless will be defiled. Is there anything more solid than a rock? Or, think, what is softer than water or drops of water? Nevertheless, the unceasing action of one element overpowers the other. Thus, if one almost unconquerable substance can be conquered by something which is nothing in comparison with it, and it suffers and is distracted, then can it be that the easily wavering human will, from the continuousness of the action, will not be defeated or corrupted?" (Letter No. 284; also in *Lives of the Saints,* Synodal ed., Moscow, 1904, under February 4).

And that is why, for the guarding of the inner man, one must strive to restrain the tongue from loquacity: *A man of understanding holdeth his peace* (Prov. 11:12), and *he that keepeth his mouth keepeth his life* (Prov. 13:3); and you remember the words of Job: *I made a covenant with mine eyes, and I will not think upon a maid* (Job 31:1), and the words of the Lord Jesus Christ: *Whosoever looketh on a woman to lust after her hath committed adultery with her already in his heart* (Matt. 5:28).

If you have not previously heard from someone concerning a certain subject, you are not obliged to answer: *He that answereth a matter before he heareth it, it is folly and shame unto him* (Prov. 18:13).

IO.

PRAYER

THOSE WHO HAVE truly decided to serve the Lord God should practice the remembrance of God and uninterrupted prayer to Jesus Christ, mentally saying: Lord Jesus Christ, Son of God, have mercy on me a sinner. In the hours after the noon meal one may say the prayer thus: Lord Jesus Christ, Son of God, by the prayers of the Mother of God, have mercy on me a sinner; or one may have recourse directly to the Most Holy Mother of God, praying: Most Holy Mother of God, save us; or one may repeat the angelic greeting: *O Theotokos and Virgin, Rejoice.* By such exercises in preserving oneself from dispersion and keeping peace of conscience one may draw near to God and be united to Him. For in the words of St. Isaac the Syrian: "Without uninterrupted prayer we cannot draw near to God" (Homily 69).

The manner of prayer was very well set forth by St. Symeon the New Theologian (*Philokalia,* "Discourse on the three manners of prayer").

The merit of this was very well described by St. John Chrysostom: "Prayer," he said, "is a great weapon, a rich treasure, a wealth that is never exhausted, an undisturbed refuge, a cause of tranquility, the root of a multitude of blessings and their source and mother" (from the Slavonic anthology *Margarit,* Discourse 5, "Concerning the Incomprehensible").

When at prayer in church it is profitable to stand with closed eyes in internal mindfulness, and to open your eyes only when you become downcast, or when sleep should weigh you down and incline you to doze; then you should fix your eyes upon an icon and the candle burning before it.

If in prayer it should happen that the mind be taken captive and its thoughts plundered, you must humble yourself before the Lord God and beg forgiveness, saying: I have sinned, Lord, by word, deed, thought, and by all my feelings.

Why one must always strive not to give oneself up to dispersion of thoughts: for through this the soul turns away from remembrance of God and love of Him through the working of the devil, as St. Macarius says: the whole concern of our enemy is this—to turn our thought away from remembrance of God, and from fear and love [of Him] (Discourse 2, ch. 15).

When the mind and heart are united in prayer and the soul's thoughts are not dispersed, the heart is warmed by spiritual warmth in which the light of Christ shines, making the whole inner man peaceful and joyous.

We should thank the Lord for everything and give ourselves up to His will; we should likewise offer Him all our thoughts, words, and strive to make everything serve only His good pleasure.

II.

TEARS

ALL SAINTS, and monks who have renounced the world, have spent their whole lives in weeping, in the hope of eternal consolation, according to the assurance of the Savior of the world: *Blessed are they that mourn (weep), for they shall be comforted* (Matt. 5:4).

And thus should we weep for the forgiveness of our sins. The words of the bearer of the purple should convince us of this: *Going they went and wept, casting their seeds; but coming they shall come with joyfulness, carrying their sheaves* (Ps. 125:6–7); as well as the words of St. Isaac the Syrian: "Moisten your cheeks with the tears of your eyes, that the Holy Spirit may abide in you, and cleanse the filth of your malice. Move your Lord with your tears, that He may help you" (Homily 68).

When we weep at prayer, and laughter mixes in, then know that this comes from the cunning of the devil. It is difficult to understand the stealthy, subtle workings of our enemy.

The heart of one who weeps tears of tender feeling *(umileniye)* is illumined by rays of the Sun of righteousness—Christ our God.

12.

SORROW

WHEN THE EVIL SPIRIT OF SORROW seizes the soul, it fills it with distress and unpleasantness, and thus it does not allow one to pray with the necessary diligence, it hinders one from reading the Scriptures with proper attention, it deprives one of meekness and deference in one's relations with the brothers, and it produces an aversion for every kind of conversation. For the soul that is filled with sorrow becomes as if mad and delirious and is unable calmly either to accept good advice or to reply meekly to questions asked of it. It flees people as if they were the cause of the sorrow and fails to understand that the cause of the affliction is within oneself. Sorrow is a worm of the heart that gnaws at the mother that gave it birth.

The sorrowing monk will not stir his mind to contemplation and can never offer pure prayer.

He who has overcome the passions has also overcome sorrow. But he who has been overcome by the passions will not escape the chains of sorrow.

As a sick man is known by the color of his face, so one who is possessed by passions is given away by his sorrow.

He who loves the world cannot but sorrow. But he who disdains the world is always joyful.

As fire purifies gold, so the sorrow of longing for God purifies a sinful heart.

13.

BOREDOM AND DESPONDENCY

AN INSEPARABLE COMPANION of the spirit of sorrow is *boredom.* It attacks a monk, as the Fathers have observed, at about midday, and it produces in him such a terrible restlessness that both the place where he lives and the brothers who live with him become unbearable to him; and during the reading there is aroused in him a kind of disgust, repeated yawning, and great hunger. Once the belly has been satisfied, the demon of boredom insinuates into the monk the idea of going out of his cell and talking to someone, suggesting that the only way of saving oneself from boredom is by constantly conversing with others. And the monk who is vanquished by boredom is like desert tumbleweed that now stops for a moment, and now is again at the mercy of the wind. He is like a wisp of cloud pursued by the wind.

This demon, if he cannot entice the monk out of his cell, begins to distract his mind during prayer and reading. This—the notion occurs to him—shouldn't be like that, and that doesn't belong here, one must put things in order; and the demon does all this in order to make the mind idle and unproductive.

This affliction is cured by prayer, abstinence from idle talk, manual labor according to one's strength, reading of the Word of God, and patience; for it is born of faintheartedness, inactivity, and idle talk (St. Isaac the Syrian, 212).

It is difficult for one just beginning the monastic life to avoid boredom, for it is the first thing to attack him. Therefore above all one must guard against it by means of strict and absolute fulfillment of all the duties laid upon the novice. When your activities fall into a real order, boredom will find no place in your heart. Only those whose affairs have no orderly arrangement are afflicted with boredom. And so obedience is the best treatment for this dangerous affliction.

When boredom vanquishes you, say to yourself, in accordance with the instructions of St. Isaac the Syrian: "You desire again an unclean and shameful life. And if the thought occurs to you: it is a great sin to kill oneself [with ascetic practices], you should say in return: I am killing myself because I cannot live uncleanly. I shall die here so as not to see real death—the death of my soul in its relation to God. It is better for me to die here in purity than to live an evil life in the world. I have preferred such a death to my sins. I am killing myself because I have sinned against God, and I will no longer anger Him. What is life to me apart from God? This affliction I will bear, so as not to be deprived of the hope of heaven. Why should God care for my life, if I live evilly and anger Him?" (Homily 22).

Boredom is one thing, and the anguish of spirit that is called *despondency* is quite another. It sometimes happens that a man is in such a spiritual state that it seems to him that it would be easier to be annihilated or to be totally without consciousness or feeling than to remain any longer in this immeasurably painful state. One must come out of it quickly. Guard yourself against the spirit of despondency, for from it comes every kind of evil (St. Barsanuphius the Great, Answer 73).

There is a natural despondency, St. Barsanuphius teaches, caused by weakness; and there is a despondency caused by a demon. They may be distinguished thus: Diabolical despondency comes before the time when one must give oneself some rest; or when someone proposes to do something, before he can finish a third or a fourth of it the demon forces him to leave the work and stand up. In such a case one should not listen to him, but should offer a prayer and patiently continue to sit and work. And the enemy, seeing that the man offers a prayer because of this, withdraws, since he does not wish to give any occasion for prayer (St. Barsanuphius the Great).

When it pleases God, says St. Isaac the Syrian, to plunge a man into greater afflictions, He permits him to fall into the hands of faintheartedness. The latter produces in him a strong force of despondency, in which he experinces a straitness of soul, and this is a foretaste of hell; as a consequence of this the spirit of delirium comes upon him, and from it thousands of temptations spring forth: anxiety, rage, blasphemy, complaining about one's lot, depraved thoughts, moving from place to place, and the like. If you will ask: what is the cause of this? then I will tell you: your negligence; because you did not take the trouble to seek a cure for them. For there is one treatment for all this, and with the aid of it a man soon finds comfort in his soul. And what kind of treatment is this? Meekness of heart. There is no way apart from this by which a man may tear down the wall of these vices; quite the contrary, he will find that they will overpower him (St. Isaac the Syrian). Despondency is sometimes called by the Holy Fathers idleness, sloth, or indolence.

14.

DESPAIR

JUST AS THE LORD is solicitous about our salvation, so too the murderer of men, the devil, strives to lead a man into despair.

A lofty and sound soul does not despair over misfortunes, of whatever sort they may be. Our life is as it were a house of temptations and trials; but we will not renounce the Lord for as long as He allows the tempter to remain with us and for as long as we must wait to be revived through patience and secure passionlessness!

Judas the betrayer was fainthearted and unskilled in battle, and so the enemy, seeing his despair, attacked him and forced him to hang himself; but Peter, a firm rock, when he fell into great sin, like one skilled in battle did not despair nor lose heart, but shed bitter tears from a burning heart, and the enemy, seeing these tears, his eyes scorched as by fire, fled far from him wailing in pain.

And so, brothers, St. Antioch teaches, when despair attacks us let us not yield to it, but being strengthened and protected by the light of faith, with great courage let us say to the evil spirit: "What are you to us, estranged from God, a fugitive from heaven and evil servant? You dare do nothing to us. Christ, the Son of God, has authority both over us and over everything. It is against Him that we have sinned, and before Him that we will be justified. And you, destroyer, leave us. Strengthened by His venerable Cross, we trample under foot your serpent's head" (St. Antioch, Discourse 27).

15.

ILLNESSES

THE BODY IS A SLAVE, the soul a sovereign, and therefore it is due to Divine mercy when the body is worn out by illness: for thereby the passions are weakened, and a man comes to himself; indeed, bodily illness itself is sometimes caused by the passions.

Take away sin, and illnesses will cease; for they occur in us because of sin, as St. Basil the Great affirms (Discourse on the truth that God is not the cause of evil): Whence come infirmities? Whence come bodily injuries? The Lord created the body, but not infirmity; the soul, but not sin. And what is above all useful and necessary? Union with God and communion with Him by means of love. If we lose this love, we fall away from Him, and in falling away we become subject to various and diverse infirmities.

Headache may be caused by agitated and excessively forced mental activity.

16.

PATIENCE AND HUMILITY

ONE SHOULD ALWAYS endure any trial for the sake of God with gratitude. Our life is a single minute in comparison with eternity; and therefore, according to the Apostle, *the sufferings of this present time are not worthy to be compared with the glory which shall be revealed in us* (Rom. 8:18).

Bear it in silence when an enemy offends you, and open your heart to the Lord.

St. Seraphim feeding the bear. Lithograph from 1903.

When anyone demeans or takes away your honor try by every means to forgive him, in accordance with the word of the Evangelist: *Of him that taketh away thy goods ask them not again* (Luke 6:30).

When men revile us, we should consider ourselves unworthy of praise. If we were worthy, everyone would bow down to us.

We should always and before everyone humble ourselves, following the teaching of St. Isaac the Syrian: Humble yourself and you will see the glory of God in yourself (Homily 57).

For this reason let us love humility and we shall see the glory of God; for where humility issues forth, there the glory of God abounds.

What is not in the light is all dark; likewise without humility there is nothing in a man but darkness alone.

17.

WORKS OF MERCY

WE SHOULD BE MERCIFUL to the needy and to travellers—the great lamps and fathers of the Church took great care over this.

We should strive by every means to fulfill the word of God: *Be ye therefore merciful, as your Father also is merciful* (Luke 6:36). And again: *I will have mercy, and not sacrifice* (Matt. 9:13).

To these saving words the wise listen, but the foolish do not listen; and therefore it is said: *He that soweth sparingly shall reap also sparingly; and he that soweth bountifully shall reap also bountifully* (II Cor. 9:6).

The example of St. Peter the Breadgiver (*Lives of the Saints,* Sept. 22), who threw bread to a poor man, can inspire us to be merciful to our neighbors.

We should do works of mercy with a good disposition of soul, according to the teaching of St. Isaac the Syrian (Homily 80): If you give to one who asks, let the joy of your countenance precede your gift, and comfort his sorrow with good words.

18.

DUTIES AND LOVE TOWARD ONE'S NEIGHBOR

WITH ONE'S NEIGHBOR one should behave kindly, giving not even the appearance of offending. When we turn away from a man or offend him, it is as though a stone were laid on the heart.

The spirit of a disturbed or desponding man one must strive to encourage by a word of love.

If a brother has sinned, cover him, as St. Isaac the Syrian advises (Homily 89): Stretch out your garment upon the one who has sinned and cover him.

We all ask the mercy of God, as the Church sings: *Had the Lord not been with us, who would have been preserved whole from the enemy, and likewise from the murderer of men?*

In relation to our neighbors we should be, both in word and in thought, pure and toward all impartial; otherwise we shall make our life unprofitable.

We should love our neighbor no less than ourselves, in accordance with the Lord's commandment: *Thou shalt love thy neighbor as thyself* (Luke 10:27). But we should not do this in such a way that love for our neighbor goes outside the boundaries of moderation and diverts us from fulfillment of the first and chief commandment, namely, the love of God. Concerning this our Lord Jesus Christ instructs us in the Gospel: *He that loveth father or mother more than Me is not worthy of Me: and he that loveth son or daughter more than Me is not worthy of Me* (Matt. 10:37).

This subject is treated quite well by St. Dimitry of Rostov (*Works,* vol. 2, Instruction 2): One may see love in a Christian man that is untrue to God where a creature is made equal to the Creator, or where a creature is revered more than the Creator; but true love may be seen where the Creator alone is loved and preferred above the whole creation.

19.

THE DUTIES OF THOSE SUBJECT TO SUPERIORS

ONE SHOULD NOT interfere in the business of those in authority and judge it; by this means one offends the majesty of God, from Whom authorities obtain their position. For *there is no power but of God; the powers that be are ordained of God* (Rom. 13:1).

One should not oppose authorities who act for good, so as not to sin before God and be subjected to His just chastisement: *Whoever resisteth the power, resisteth the ordinance of God; and they that resist shall receive to themselves damnation* (Rom. 13:2).

One must be in obedience to a superior: for through this he who is obedient prospers mightily in the formation of his soul; and in addition he obtains by this means an understanding of things and comes to heartfelt contrition.

20.

DO NOT JUDGE YOUR NEIGHBOR

WE MUST NOT JUDGE anyone, even if with our own eyes we have seen someone sinning, or walking in transgression of God's commandments. For according to the word of God: *Judge not, that ye be not judged* (Matt. 7:1), and again: *Who art thou that judgest another man's servant? To his own master he standeth or falleth; yea, he shall be holden up: for God is able to make him stand* (Rom. 14:4).

It is much better always to bring to mind these words of the Apostle: *Let him that thinketh he standeth take heed lest he fall* (I Cor. 10:12).

For we do not know how long we may remain in virtue, as says the Prophet who attained to knowledge of this matter by experience: *In my prosperity I said, I shall never be moved. Thou didst hide Thy face, and I am troubled* (Ps. 29:7, 8).

21.

FORGIVENESS OF OFFENSES

FOR AN OFFENCE, whatever kind may have been given, one must not only not avenge oneself, but on the contrary must all the more forgive from the heart, even though it may resist this, and must incline the heart by conviction of the word of God: *If ye forgive not men their trespasses, neither will your Father forgive your trespasses* (Matt. 6:15); and again, *Pray for them which despitefully use you* (Matt. 5:44).

One must not nurse in one's heart malice or hatred towards a neighbor who bears ill-will; but we must strive to love him and, as much as possible, do good, following the teaching of our Lord Jesus Christ: *Love your enemies, do good to them that hate you* (Matt. 5:44).

And thus, if we will strive, as much as lies in our power, to fulfill all this, then we may hope that Divine light will shine early in our souls, opening to us the path to the Jerusalem on High.

22.

CARE FOR THE SOUL

MAN, AS FAR AS his body is concerned, is like a lighted candle. A candle must be consumed; thus also the body must die. But the soul is immortal, and so our care also must be more for the soul than for the body: *For what shall it profit a man, if he shall gain the whole world, and lose his own soul?* (Mark 8:36).

Sts. Basil the Great, Gregory the Theologian, John Chrysostom, Cyril of Alexandria, Ambrose of Milan, and others, from their youth to the end of their life were virgins: their whole life was devoted to care for the soul, and not for the body. Thus our whole endeavor too should be for the soul; the body should be strengthened only so that it might aid in the strengthening of the spirit.

If we willfully exhaust our body to the point where the spirit also is exhausted, such an oppression will be foolish, even though it were done for the acquiring of virtue.

But if it be pleasing to the Lord God that a man undergo illnesses, He will give him also strength to endure.

And so let illnesses be not from us ourselves, but from God.

23.

WITH WHAT SHOULD ONE NOURISH THE SOUL?

ONE SHOULD NOURISH the soul with the word of God: for the word of God, as St. Gregory the Theologian says, is angelic bread, by which are nourished souls that hunger for God. Most of all one should occupy oneself with reading the New Testament and the Psalter, which one should do standing up. From this there occurs an enlightenment in the mind, which is changed by a Divine change.

One should habituate oneself in this way so that the mind might as it were swim in the Lord's law; it is under the guidance of this law that one should direct one's life.

It is very profitable to occupy oneself with reading the word of God in solitude, and to read the whole Bible intelligently. For one such occupation alone, apart from good deeds, the Lord will not leave a person without His mercy, but will fill him with the gift of understanding.

And when a man nourishes his soul with the word of God, there is realized [in him] an understanding of what is good and what evil.

The reading of the word of God should be performed in solitude, in order that the whole mind of the reader might be plunged into the truths of the Holy Scripture, and that from this he might receive warmth, which in solitude produces tears; from these a man is wholly warmed and is filled with spiritual gifts, which rejoice the mind and heart more than any word.

One should likewise nourish the soul also with knowledge of the Church: how she has been preserved from the beginning up to the present, what she has endured in one or another time; but one should know this not so as to desire to direct people, but in case one should encounter powerful opposition.

Most of all one should do this strictly for oneself, so as to acquire peace of soul, according to the teaching of the Psalmist: *Great peace have those who love Thy law, O Lord* (Ps. 118:165).

24.

PEACE OF SOUL

NOTHING IS BETTER than peace in Christ; in it is destroyed every warfare of the spirits of the air and earth: *For we wrestle not against flesh and blood, but against principalities, against powers, against the rulers of the darkness of this world, against spiritual wickedness in high places* (Eph. 6:12).

It is the mark of a wise soul when a man plunges his mind within himself and has activity in his heart.

Then the grace of God overshadows him, and he is in a peaceful state, and by means of this also in a most peaceful state: peaceful, that is, with a good conscience; and most peaceful, for the mind beholds within itself the grace of the Holy Spirit, according to the word of God: *And His place is in peace* (Ps. 75:3).

Can one, seeing the sun with one's sensuous eyes, not rejoice? But how much more joyful it is when the mind sees with its inner eye the Sun of justice, Christ! Then in truth one rejoices with angelic joy; of this the Apostle too said: *Our conversation is in heaven* (Phil. 3:20).

When one walks in a peaceful state, it is as if one ladles out spiritual gifts with a spoon.

The Holy Fathers, being in a peaceful state and being overshadowed by Divine grace, lived long.

When a man enters into a peaceful state, he can give out from himself and also upon others light for the enlightenment of the mind; but before this a man must repeat these words of the prophetess (Hannah): *Let not high-sounding words come out of your mouth* (I Kings [Samuel] 2:3), and the words of the

Lord: *Thou hypocrite, first cast out the beam out of thine own eye; and then shalt thou see clearly to cast out the mote out of thy brother's eye* (Matt. 7:5).

This peace, like some priceless treasure, our Lord Jesus Christ left to His disciples before His death, saying: *Peace I leave with you, My peace I give unto you* (John 14:27). Of it the Apostle likewise speaks: *And the peace of God, which passeth all understanding, shall keep your hearts and minds through Christ Jesus* (Phil. 4:7).

And so we must concentrate all our thoughts, desires, and actions in order to receive the peace of God and to cry out ever with the Church: *O Lord our God, give us peace* (Is. 26:12).

25.

PRESERVING PEACE OF SOUL

ONE MUST BY EVERY MEANS strive to preserve peace of soul and not to be disturbed by offenses from others; for this one must in every way strive to restrain anger and by means of attentiveness to keep the mind and heart from improper feelings.

And therefore we must bear offenses from others with equanimity and accustom ourselves to such a disposition of spirit that these offenses seem to concern not us, but others.

Such a practice can give quietness to the human heart and make it a dwelling for God Himself.

An example of such angerlessness we see in St. Gregory the Wonderworker, from whom a certain prostitute in a public place asked recompense, as if for a sin he had committed with her; and he, not becoming in the least angry with her, meekly said to a certain friend of his: give her quickly the sum she demands. The woman had no sooner taken the unjust recompense than she was subjected to the attack of a demon; and the saint drove the demon out of her by prayer (*Lives of Saints,* Nov. 17).

If, however, it is impossible not to be disturbed, then at least one must strive to restrain the tongue, according to the Psalmist: *I was troubled, and spoke not* (Ps. 76:5).

43

St. Seraphim in the forest. From *The Diveyevo Chronicles.*

In this case we may take as an example Sts. Spyridon of Tremithus and Ephraim the Syrian. The first (*Lives of Saints,* Dec. 12) bore an offense thus: When, at the demand of the Greek Emperor, he entered the Palace, one of the servants who had been in the Emperor's chamber, taking him for a beggar, burst out laughing at him, did not allow him into the chambers, and then hit him on the cheek. St. Spyridon, being gentle, in accordance with the word of the Lord, turned the other to him also (cf. Matt. 5:39). St. Ephraim (*Lives of Saints,* Jan. 28), while fasting in the wilderness, was deprived of food by a disciple in this fashion: The disciple, carrying food to him, accidentally shattered the dish on the way. The saint, seeing the sorrowing disciple, said to him: Do not be sad, brother; if the food did not desire to come to us, then we will go to it. And he went, sat down beside the shattered dish and, gathering the food, ate it: so without anger was he.

And in what fashion to vanquish anger one may see from the Life of St. Paisius the Great (*Lives of Saints,* June 19), who asked the Lord Jesus Christ, Who had appeared to him, to free him from anger; and Christ said to him: If you wish to vanquish anger and rage together, desire nothing, neither hate anyone nor belittle anyone.

In order to preserve peace of soul, one must remove from oneself despondency and strive to have a joyful spirit and not a sad one, according to the word of Sirach: *For sorrow has killed many, and there is no profit therein* (Sirach, or Ecclesiasticus, 30:23).

When a man has a great insufficiency of those things needed for the body, it is difficult to vanquish despondency. But this, of course, is applicable to weak souls.

For the preservation of peace of soul one must likewise by every means flee from judgment of others. By not judging and by silence peace of soul is maintained: when a man is in such a state, he receives Divine revelations.

In order to free oneself from judging, one must take heed of oneself, not to accept outside thoughts from anyone and to be dead to everything.

For the preservation of peace of soul one must more often enter into oneself and ask: where am I?

At the same time one must watch that the bodily senses, especially sight, serve for the inner man and do not distract the soul by means of sensuous objects: for they only receive grace-bearing gifts who have interior activity and are vigilant over their souls.

26.

GUARDING THE HEART

WE MUST VIGILANTLY guard our heart from unfitting thoughts and impressions, according to the word of the writer of Proverbs: *Keep thine heart with the utmost care; for out of these are the issues of life* (Prov. 4:23).

From constant guarding of the heart purity is born in it, purity in which is beheld the Lord, according to the assurance of eternal Truth: *Blessed are the pure in heart, for they shall see God* (Matt. 5:8).

Whatever of that which is best has flowed into the heart, we should not pour out without need: for that which has been gathered can be free of danger from visible and invisible enemies only when it is guarded in the interior of the heart.

The heart boils, being kindled by Divine fire, only when there is living water in it; but when this is poured out, it grows cold and a man freezes.

27.

DISCERNMENT OF THE HEART'S WORKINGS

WHEN A MAN RECEIVES something Divine, in his heart he rejoices; but when he receives something diabolic, he is disturbed.

The Christian heart, when it has received something Divine, does not demand anything else in order to convince it that this is precisely from the Lord; but by that very effect it is convinced that this is heavenly, for it senses within itself spiritual fruits: *love, joy, peace,* and the rest (Gal. 5:22).

On the contrary, though the devil might transform himself even *into an angel of light* (II Cor. 11:14), or might produce thoughts seemingly good: still the heart would feel a certain obscureness and agitation in its thoughts. Explaining this, St. Macarius of Egypt says: Though satan might produce also visions of light, he is entirely unable to produce a blessed effect: which is the well-known sign of his works (St. Macarius, Homily 4, ch. 13).

And thus, from these diverse workings of the heart a man may know what is Divine and what diabolic, as St. Gregory the Sinaite writes: From the effect one may know whether the light shining in one's soul is of God or of satan.

28.

THE LIGHT OF CHRIST

TO RECEIVE AND BEHOLD in the heart the light of Christ, one must, as far as possible, divert one's attention away from visible objects. Having purified the soul beforehand by repentance and good deeds, and with faith in the Crucified, having closed the bodily eyes, immerse the mind within the heart, in which place cry out with the invocation of the name of our Lord Jesus Christ; and then, to the measure of one's zeal and warmth of spirit toward the Beloved, a man finds in the invoked name a delight which awakens the desire to seek higher illumination.

When through such a practice the mind enters into the heart, the light of Christ shines, illuminating the chamber of the soul by its Divine radiance, as the Prophet Malachi says: *But unto you that fear My name, the Sun of justice shall arise* (Mal. 4:2).

This light is likewise life, according to the word of the Gospel: *In Him was life, and the life was the light of men* (John 1:4).

When a man beholds the eternal light interiorly, his mind is pure and has in it no sensory representations, but, being totally immersed in contemplation of uncreated goodness, he forgets everything sensory and wishes not even to see himself; he desires rather to hide himself in the heart of the earth, if only he be not deprived of this true good—God.

29.

ON THOUGHTS AND MOVEMENTS OF THE FLESH

IF WE DO NOT AGREE with the evil thoughts suggested by the devil, we do good.

The impure spirit has a strong influence only on the passionate, while upon those who have purified themselves of passions he attacks only from the side, or exteriorly.

Is it possible for a man in his youth to burn and not be disturbed by fleshly thoughts? But one should pray to the Lord God that the spark of impure passions may be extinguished at the very beginning. Then the flame of passions will not increase in a man.

30.

HEEDFULNESS TO ONESELF

HE WHO IS TRAVELING the path of heedfulness should not trust only his own heart, but should verify the workings of his heart and his life with the law of God and with the active life of ascetics of piety who passed through such endeavor. By this means one may the more easily both save oneself from the evil one and more clearly behold the truth.

The mind of a heedful man is as it were a watchman on duty, or an unsleeping guard of the inner Jerusalem. Standing at the height of spiritual contemplation, he looks with an eye of purity upon the enemy powers who go around and attack his soul, in accordance with the Psalmist: *And my eye hath looked down upon my enemies* (Ps. 53:9).

From his eye the devil is not hidden, who *as a roaring lion walketh about seeking whom he may devour* (I Peter 5:8), nor are they who bend their bow *to shoot in the dark the upright of heart* (Ps. 10:2).

And thus such a man, following the teaching of the divine Paul, receives *the whole armor of God, that [he] may be able to withstand in the evil day* (Eph.

6:13), and with this armor and with the cooperating grace of God, he repels visible attacks and vanquishes invisible warriors.

He who travels this path should not heed extraneous reports, from which the head can be filled with idle and vain thoughts and recollections; but he should be heedful toward himself.

Especially on this path one must watch lest one turn to the affairs of others, lest one think or speak of them, according to the Psalmist: *That my mouth may not speak of the works of men* (Ps. 16:4); but one should pray to the Lord: *From my secret [sins] cleanse me, and from those of others spare Thy servant* (Ps. 18:13–14).

A man should turn his attention to the beginning and end of his life; however, toward the middle part, where occur fortunes or misfortunes, he should be indifferent.

To preserve heedfulness one must retire into oneself, according to the word of the Lord: *Salute no man by the way* (Luke 10:4), i.e., do not speak without need, unless someone run after you to hear from you something profitable.

Revere elders or brethren whom you meet with bows, having your eyes always closed.

31.

AGAINST TOO GREAT SOLICITUDE

TOO GREAT SOLICITUDE for worldly things is natural to an unbelieving and fainthearted man. And woe to us if we, in taking care for ourselves, do not confirm ourselves in our hope in God, Who takes care for us! If we do not ascribe to Him the visible goods which we use in this present age, how can we expect from Him those goods which are promised in the future? Let us not be such faint believers, but rather let us *seek first the Kingdom of God, and all these things shall be added* unto us, according to the word of the Savior (Matt. 6:33).

It is better for us to despise what is not ours, *i.e.,* the temporal and passing, and desire our own, *i.e.,* incorruption and immortality. For when we shall be incorruptible and immortal, we shall become worthy of visible contemplation of God, like the Apostles at the most divine Transfiguration, and we shall be joined in a union with God surpassing the mind, like the heavenly minds. For we shall be like the angels, and sons of God, *being the sons of the resurrection* (Luke 20:36).

32.

RENUNCIATION OF THE WORLD

FEAR OF GOD IS ACQUIRED when a man, renouncing the world and everything that is in the world, concentrates all his thoughts and feelings on the single thought of God's law, and immerses himself entirely in contemplation of God and in a feeling of the blessedness promised to the saints.

One cannot renounce the world and come into a state of spiritual contemplation while remaining in the world. For as long as the passions are not quieted, one cannot acquire peace of soul. But the passions do not become quiet as long as we are surrounded by the objects which awaken the passions. In order to come into perfect passionlessness and attain perfect silence of the soul, one must labor much in spiritual reflection and prayer. But how is it possible fully and calmly to immerse oneself in contemplation of God, and be instructed in His law, and ascend with all one's soul to Him in flaming prayer, while remaining amidst the perpetual roar of passions warring in the world? The world lies in evil.

Without having freed itself from the world, the soul cannot love God sincerely. For worldly things, in the words of St. Antioch, are as it were a veil for the soul.

If, says the same teacher, we live in an alien city and our city is far from this city, and if we know our city: then why do we tarry in an alien city and prepare for ourselves a field and a dwelling in it? And how shall we sing a song to the Lord in an alien land? This world is the domain of another, *i.e.,* the prince of this world (Homily 15).

33.

ASCETIC LABORS

ONE SHOULD NOT undertake ascetic labors beyond one's measure, but one should strive to make our friend—the flesh—faithful and capable of performing virtues.

One should go by a middle path: *turn not aside to the right hand nor to the left* (Prov. 4:27); and one should render unto the spirit what is spiritual, and unto the body what is bodily; for the maintenance of temporal life, one should render what is necessary, and for life in society, that which is lawfully demanded by it, in accordance with the words of Holy Scripture: *Render unto Caesar the things that are Caesar's, and unto God the things that are God's* (Matt. 22:21).

One must condescend to the soul in its infirmities and imperfections, and bear its defects as we bear those of others; one must not, however, become lazy, but should spur oneself to do better.

Perhaps one has eaten too much, or done something similar to this which is natural to human weakness—do not be disturbed at this, and do not add injury to injury; but bestir yourself to correction and at the same time strive to preserve peace of soul, according to the word of the Apostle: *Blessed is he that condemneth not himself in that thing which he alloweth* (Rom. 14:22).

The same thought is contained in the words of the Savior: *Except ye be converted, and become as little children, ye shall not enter into the kingdom of heaven* (Matt. 18:3).

If the body has been worn out by ascetic labors or sickness, one should strengthen it with moderate sleep, food and drink, not observing even the times. Jesus Christ, after the raising of Jairus' daughter, immediately commanded: *Give her to eat* (Luke 8:55).

Every success in anything we should refer to the Lord and with the Prophet say: *Not to us, O Lord, not to us, but to Thy name give glory* (Ps. 113:9).

To the age of about 35, that is, to the midpoint of our earthly life, it is a great accomplishment for a man to preserve himself, and many in these years do not remain in virtue, but turn aside from the right path to their own desires; thus St. Basil testifies of this (Homily on the beginning of Proverbs): Many have gathered much in their youth, but being in the midst of life they could not bear the tumult of temptations which rose up against them from the spirit of cunning, and they were deprived of all this.

And therefore, in order not to experience such a metamorphosis, one must put oneself as it were on the scale of a test and an attentive self-examination, according to the teaching of St. Isaac the Syrian: For as on a scale it is fitting that the destiny of each be weighed out (Homily 40, On Prayer).

34.

REPENTANCE

H E WHO WOULD BE SAVED should ever have his heart disposed to repentance and broken, according to the Psalmist: *A sacrifice to God is a broken spirit: a broken and humbled heart God will not despise* (Ps. 50:17).

In such brokenness of spirit a man can easily pass securely through the artful snares of the proud devil, whose whole care consists in agitating the human spirit, and in agitation sowing his tares, in accordance with the words of the Gospel: *Lord, didst not thou sow good seed in thy field? From whence then hath it tares? He said unto them, An enemy hath done this* (Matt. 13:27–28).

When, however, a man strives within himself to have his heart humble and his thought not agitated, but peaceful, then all the snares of the enemy are without effect; for where there is peace in one's thoughts, there resides the Lord God Himself—*His place is in peace* (Ps. 75:3).

The beginning of repentance proceeds from fear of God and heedfulness, as the holy Martyr Boniface says (*Lives of Saints,* Dec. 19): The fear of God is the father of heedfulness, and heedfulness is the mother of inner peace, and the latter gives birth to conscience, which causes the soul to behold its own ugliness as in a certain pure and undisturbed water; and thus are born the beginnings and roots of repentance.

Throughout our whole life by our transgressions we offend in greater or less degree the majesty of God, and therefore we should also ever humble ourselves before Him, begging remission of our debts.

Question: Can a man who has received grace rise after falling?

Answer: He can, according to the Psalmist, *I was overturned that I might fall, but the Lord supported me* (Ps. 117:13); for when Nathan the prophet accused David in his sin, the latter repented and immediately received forgiveness (II Kings 12:13).

An example of the same thing may be found in the anchorite who, going for water, fell into sin with a woman at the spring, and returning to his cell, acknowledged his sin and began again to lead an ascetic life as before, not accepting the counsel of the enemy who represented to him the seriousness of the sin and would have led him away from the ascetic life. The Lord revealed this incident to a certain father, and commanded him to glorify the brother who had fallen into sin for such a victory over the devil.

35.

FASTING

TO LAY UPON ONESELF a strict rule of abstinence in everything, or to deprive oneself of everything that might serve to lighten one's weaknesses—not everyone can accept this.

One should partake of enough food every day so that the body, strengthened, may be the friend and helper of the soul in the performance of virtue; otherwise it way happen that, while wearing out one's body, one's soul also will grow weak.

On Fridays and Wednesdays, and especially during the four fasts, partake of food once in the day, and an angel of the Lord will join himself to you.

36.

VIGILANCE AGAINST TEMPTATIONS

O NE SHOULD, as far as it is proper and necessary, be sometimes a child, and sometimes a lion, this latter especially when passions or evil spirits rise up against us; because *we wrestle not against flesh and blood, but against principalities, against powers, against the rulers of the darkness of this world, against spiritual wickedness in high places* (Eph. 6:12).

We must always be attentive to the assaults of the devil; for can we hope that he will leave us without temptation, when he did not leave our Founder and Source of faith and Perfecter the Lord Jesus Christ Himself? The Lord Himself said to the Apostle Peter: *Simon, Simon, behold, satan hath desired to have you, that he may sift you as wheat* (Luke 22:31).

And thus we must ever call upon the Lord in humility and pray that He may not allow us to be tempted beyond our strength, but that He may deliver us from the evil one.

For when the Lord leaves a man to himself, the devil is ready to grind him, as a millstone grinds kernels of wheat.

37.

SOLITUDE AND SILENCE

M ORE THAN ANYTHING ELSE one should adorn oneself with si- lence; for St. Ambrose of Milan says: I have seen many being saved by silence, but not one by talkativeness. And again one of the Fathers says that silence is the mystery of the future age, while words are the implement of this world (St. Isaac the Syrian).

Only sit in your cell in heedfulness and silence, and by every means strive to draw near to the Lord, and the Lord is ready to transform you from a man into an angel, *and to whom,* He says, *will I look, but to him that is meek and silent, and that trembleth at My words?* (Is. 66:2).

When we remain in silence, our enemy the devil will have no success with regard to a man with a hidden heart; by this, however, must be understood silence in the mind.

One who goes through such an ascetic endeavor should place all his hope on the Lord God, in accordance with the teaching of the Apostle: *Casting all your care upon Him, for He careth for you* (I Peter 5:7).

Such a one should be constant in this ascetic endeavor, following in this case the example of St. John the Silent One and Anchorite (*Lives of Saints,* Dec. 3), who in the traversing of this path strengthened himself with these Divine words: *I will not leave thee, neither will I forsake thee* (Heb. 13:5).

If one cannot always remain in solitude and silence while living in a monastery and occupying oneself with the obediences placed upon one by the superior, then at least a little time that is left after obediences should be devoted to solitude and silence, and for this little the Lord God will not neglect to send down His grace-giving mercy.

From solitude and silence are born tender contrition* and meekness; the activity of this latter in the human heart may be compared to that quiet water of Siloe, which flows without noise or sound, as the Prophet Isaiah speaks of it: *the waters of Siloe that go softly* (Is. 8:6).

Remaining in one's cell in silence, work, prayer, and instruction day and night in God's law, makes a man pious; for, in the words of the Holy Fathers, the cell of a monk is the Babylonian furnace, and in it the three youths found the Son of God (St. Peter of Damascus, *Philokalia*).

38.

ABSOLUTE SILENCE

ABSOLUTE SILENCE is a cross upon which a man must crucify himself with all the passions and desires. But only think, how much our master Christ suffered beforehand slanders and offenses, and only then ascended the Cross.

---

* *Umileniye* in Russian.

Thus we too cannot enter into absolute silence and hope for holy perfection if we do not suffer with Christ. For, says the Apostle: *If so be that we suffer with Him, that we may be also glorified with Him* (Rom. 8:17). There is no other path (St. Barsanuphius, Answer 342).

He who has entered into silence must unfailingly keep in mind why he has done so, in order that his heart may not be turned away to something else.

39.

THE ACTIVE AND THE CONTEMPLATIVE LIFE

MAN IS COMPOSED of soul and body, and therefore his life's path also should consist of activities of the body and of the soul—of action and mental contemplation.

The path of the active life consists of: fasting, continence, vigils, prostrations, prayer and other bodily ascetic labors, which comprise the narrow and grievous path which, according to God's word, leads to eternal life (cf. Matt. 7:14).

The path of the contemplative life consists of the elevation of the mind to the Lord God, of heartfelt heedfulness, mental prayer, and, through such practices, contemplation of spiritual things.

Everyone who desires to traverse the spiritual life must begin with the active life, and only then come to the contemplative: for without the active life it is impossible to enter the contemplative.

The active life serves to cleanse us of sinful passions, and it leads us up to the stage of active perfection; and by this very means it paves for us the path to the contemplative life. For only those who have been cleansed of passions and are perfect can approach that life, as one may see from the words of Holy Scripture: *Blessed are the pure in heart, for they shall see God* (Matt. 5:8), and from the words of St. Gregory the Theologian (in his sermon for Holy Pascha): Only those most perfect by their experience approach without danger to contemplation.

One should approach the contemplative life with fear and trembling, with contrition of heart and humility, with much experience of the Holy Scriptures, and, if one can find him, under the direction of some experienced elder; and not with audacity and self-esteem. For he who is audacious and disdainful, in the words of St. Gregory the Sinaite (*Philokalia*), having sought with pride for something beyond his worth, is compelled to think he is ready for it prematurely. And again: If anyone imagines in conceit to attain something high, this is a satanic desire, and, without acquiring truth, he will be handily seized by the devil with his nets, as his servant.

But if one cannot find an instructor able to direct one into the contemplative life, in this case one must be directed by the Holy Scripture, for the Lord Himself commands us to learn from Holy Scripture, saying: *Search the Scriptures, for in them ye think ye have eternal life* (John 5:39).

Likewise one must endeavor to read through the writings of the Fathers, and strive as much as possible, according to one's strength, to fulfill what they teach, and in this fashion, little by little ascend from the active life to the perfection of the contemplative.

For in the words of St. Gregory the Theologian (Sermon on Holy Pascha), it is the very best deed when we each attain perfection ourselves. To God, Who calls us, we must offer to God a sacrifice living and holy, always and in everything being sanctified.

A man must not leave the active life even when he may have had success in it and have already entered the contemplative life, for it cooperates with the contemplative life and elevates it.

Traversing the path of the interior and contemplative life, one must not relax and leave it because people, having become attached to exterior and sensual things, strike us a blow in the very heart's feeling by the opposition of their opinions, and strive by every means to turn us aside from the traversing of the interior path, placing in our path various obstacles; for, in the opinion of the teachers of the Church (Blessed Theodoret, Commentary on the Song of Songs), the contemplation of spiritual things is preferred to the knowledge of sensual things.

And therefore one must not waver over any obstacles to the traversing of this path, strengthening oneself in this case with the word of God: *But let us fear not their fear, neither let us be dismayed: for God is with us. Let us sanctify the Lord God Himself in heartfelt remembrance of His Divine name and fulfillment of His will, and He shall be our fear* (Is. 8:12, 13).

40.

INSTRUCTION TO A NOVICE

WHETHER BY someone's advice, or by the authority of others, or by whatever other means you came to this monastery, do not fall into despondency: this is God's visitation to you. If you observe that which has been told you, you will be saved yourself together with your close ones whom you care for: *I have not seen,* said the Prophet, *the righteous forsaken, nor his seed* (Ps. 36:25). Living, then, in this monastery, observe this: standing in church, be attentive to everything without neglect, learn the whole order of the Church services, *i.e.,* Vespers, Compline, Nocturns, Matins, the Hours; learn to keep them in the mind.

If you are in your cell without any work for the hands, be diligent in all kinds of reading, but above all in the reading of the Psalter; strive to read each section many times, so as to keep all in the mind. If there is work for the hands, occupy yourself with it; if you are called to an obedience, go to it. At handiwork, or being anywhere at an obedience, constantly say the prayer: Lord Jesus Christ, Son of God, have mercy on me, a sinner. At prayer pay heed to yourself, *i.e.,* gather the mind and unite it with the soul. At the beginning for a day, then for two and many, say this prayer with the mind alone, each time separately, paying particular attention to each word. Then, when the Lord will kindle your heart with the warmth of His grace and will unite it within you into a single spirit: then this prayer will flow within you ceaselessly and will always be with you, delighting and nourishing you. It is this very thing that is spoken of by the Prophet Isaiah: *For the dew from Thee is healing to them* (Is. 26:19).

And when you will hold within yourself this nourishment for the soul, *i.e.,* this conversation with the Lord Himself, then why would you go to the cells of the brethren, even though you may be called by someone? I tell you truly that this is idle talk and love of idleness. If you do not understand yourself, can you reason about anything else and teach others? Be silent, be ceaselessly silent; keep always in mind the presence of God and His name. Enter into conversation with no one, but by every means guard against judging those who speak much or laugh. Be in this case deaf and dumb; no matter what may be said about you, let it pass by your ears. As your example you can take St. Stephen the New (*Lives of Saints,* Nov. 28), whose prayer was ceaseless, his disposition meek, his mouth silent, his heart humble, his spirit filled with tender feeling (*umileniye*), his body and soul pure, his virginity immaculate, whose true poverty and whose non-acquisitiveness were unmurmuring, his obedience thorough, his execution patient and his labor diligent.

Sitting at meals, do not look and do not judge how much anyone eats, but be attentive to yourself, nourishing your soul with prayer. At dinner eat sufficiently, at supper restrain yourself. On Wednesdays and Fridays, if you are able, eat once a day. Every day without fail sleep four hours at night: the 10th, 11th, and 12th, and the hour past midnight [*i.e.,* from 9:00 p.m. to 1:00 a.m.]; if you become weak, you can sleep more in the afternoon. Hold to this unfailingly to the end of your life: for this is necessary to give rest to your head. I, also, from my youth have held to such a path. And we always beg the Lord God to give us repose at night-time. If you will guard yourself thus, you will not be despondent but healthy and joyful.

I tell you in truth, that if you will conduct yourself thus, you will remain in the monastery without leaving to your death. Humble yourself, and the Lord will help you, *and He shall bring forth thy righteousness as the light, and thy judgment as the noonday* (Ps. 36:6), and thy *light* will *shine before men* (Matt. 5:16).

41.

REPLY TO A BROTHER WHO ASKED INSTRUCTION ON LEADING AN ANCHORITIC LIFE

ONE BROTHER, when he had the intent to go away into the wilderness, came to Fr. Seraphim, who was living in the wilderness, and asked him: How is it, Father, that some say that going away from coenobitic life into the wilderness is Phariseeism, and that by such means one shows disdain for the brethren or even judgment of them? Fr. Seraphim replied to this: It is not our business to judge others, and we go away from the brotherhood not out of hatred for it, but rather because we have accepted and bear on ourselves the angelic habit, to which it is not fitting to be in a place where by word and deed the Lord God is angered. And therefore we, excluding ourselves from the brotherhood, go away only from hearing and seeing that which is opposed to God's commandments, which happens in many of the brethren. We do not flee men, who are of one nature with us and bear one and the same name of Christ; but we flee the faults which they commit, as was said also to Arsenius the Great: Flee men, and you will be saved (*Lives of Saints,* May 8).

One monk was blessed by the abbot to begin an anchoritic life, and the abbot wrote to Fr. Seraphim asking him to receive this monk and discipline him as he himself would. When this monk came with such a letter to Fr. Seraphim, the latter received him quite kindly, and blessed him to build another cell not so far from his own. When, however, this monk began to ask instruction of him, he told him, out of the deepest humility, that "I myself don't know anything," and he reminded him of the words of the Savior: *Learn of Me, for I am meek and lowly in heart: and ye shall find rest unto your souls* (Matt. 11:29). Then he added: In the opinion of St. John of the Ladder, we should learn, not from an angel or a man, but from the Lord Himself.

42.

WHAT AN ABBOT SHOULD BE

AN ABBOT SHOULD BE PERFECT in every virtue and have the senses of his soul trained by long schooling in the discernment of good and evil (Heb. 5:14).

An abbot should be well versed in the Holy Scripture; he should be studying day and night in the Lord's law. Through such occupations he may acquire for himself the gift of discerning good and evil.

A true understanding of good and evil may be had only when an ascetic of piety comes to a sense of the future judgment and a foretaste of eternal blessedness, which occurs in a pious soul while yet in this present earthly life, in a mysterious and spiritual manner.

Before coming to the discernment of good and evil, a man is not fit to shepherd rational sheep, but only irrational ones; because without the understanding of good and evil we cannot comprehend the workings of the evil one.

And therefore an abbot, as a pastor of rational sheep, must also have the gift of discernment, so that in each case he could give useful advice to everyone asking his instructions; for, as Peter of Damascus says (in the *Philokalia*), not every man is fit to give advice to those who seek, but he who has received from God the gift of discernment and from long experience in ascetic life has acquired a perspicacious mind.

An abbot should also have the gift of penetrativeness, so that from the consideration of things present and past he may foresee those future as well, and see through the wiles of the enemy.

The distinguishing characteristic of an abbot should be his love for those subject to him: for a genuine shepherd, in the words of St. John of the Ladder, is revealed by his love for his flock, for love compelled the Supreme Shepherd to be crucified on the Cross (in his book *To the Shepherd,* chapter 5).

43.

INSTRUCTION TO AN ABBOT ON HOW
TO DIRECT THE BRETHREN

A CERTAIN ABBOT, being by chance in Sarov Monastery, when meeting Fr. Seraphim asked his advice on how to direct the brethren. Fr. Seraphim gave him the following instruction:

Let every abbot become and remain always in his relation to those subject to him as a wise mother.

A mother who loves her children lives not to satisfy herself, but to satisfy her children. The infirmities of her infirm children she bears with love:

those who have fallen into filth she cleans, washes them calmly, clothes them in new white garments, puts their shoes on, warms them, feeds them, looks after them, comforts them, and from all sides strives to pacify their spirit so that she never hears the slightest cry from them; and such children are well disposed to their mother. Thus should every abbot live not to satisfy himself, but to satisfy those subject to him—he should be condescending to their weaknesses; bear with love the infirmities of the infirm; heal their sinful diseases with the plaster of mercifulness; raise with kindness those who have fallen into transgressions; quietly cleanse those who have become sullied with the filth of some vice and wash them by placing upon them fasting and prayer above the ordinary amount which is set forth for all; clothe them, by instruction and by one's own exemplary life, in garments of virtues; keep constant watch over them; by every means comforting them, and from all sides defend their peace and repose to such an extent that the slightest cry or murmuring will never be heard from them; and then they will zealously strive to procure for the abbot peace and repose.

With this the Spiritual Instructions *of St. Seraphim end.*
Glory to our God!

II

The Acquisition of the Holy Spirit

Nicholas Alexandrovich Motovilov.

EDITOR'S PREFACE

THE CONVERSATION of our holy and God-bearing Father Seraphim, Wonderworker of Sarov, on the aim of the Christian life has great significance; it is perhaps the most important thing that we have about him.

It was set forth as a theological instruction by one of the great saints of the Orthodox Church, comparable to the Holy Fathers of antiquity. As something genuine, remaining as a testimony of the holiness of a great righteous one of the Russian Church, it is clearly a revelation from above. The absolutely extraordinary finding occurred just before the glorification of the great seer of mysteries. Absolutely striking is the significance of this teaching "which has come from the other world," as if it were foreordained for the Christians of the 20th century! It is also amazing to consider who was granted to acquire this wonderful treasure and under what circumstances it was proclaimed throughout all classes of great Russia, precisely on the eve of the historic disappearance of Holy Russia from this earth....

And we have been entrusted to transmit it still further, to all peoples of the world, to whoever "has ears to hear" and a heart prepared to receive the flaming words of Truth itself, which proceeded from the lips of this veritable heavenly seraph—our most precious and dear Batiushka Serakhvim.*

Although the miracle of the appearance of this seraph to our sinful earth lives until this day and breathes in our church life, it has still not said its final word; it is still unfinished. St. Seraphim is the inheritance of the Universal Church of Christ, the One and Genuine. Concluding his Conversation, the saint says to Motovilov, his fellow converser:

---

* "Batiushka" is an endearing way of saying "Father." St. Seraphim pronounced his name "Serakh-vim," according to the dialect of the Kursk region.

"The Lord will help you ever to retain this [teaching on the Holy Spirit] in your memory … moreover, since it is not given for you alone to understand it, but through you for the entire world…." The saint has yet to appear to many who do not know him and to those in darkness, whose hearts have not yet been set aflame by divine love, that they might make through him a decisive choice, before the last trumpet sounds…. But at a quick pace iniquity veils our sinful earth; and evidently her end will be soon, for the tidings about St. Seraphim have spread from Russia to the world abroad.

This conversation was found by Sergei Alexandrovich Nilus. He was a fascinating man. It was not in vain that the saint chose him as it were to be a new "servant of poor Seraphim"; and he in actual fact did serve the saint through the publication of the Conversation, as well as through his literary labors in general. Below we present the complete text from the third and last printing of the Conversation, which was corrected by Nilus and provided by him with a foreword, afterword and notes hitherto unpublished. The Conversation constitutes one of the chapters of his first, and extremely interesting, book *Greatness in Small Things,* dedicated "with feeling of devout appreciation" to the wondrous healer himself, the holy Righteous Father John of Kronstadt.

Gleb Podmoshensky
Summer 1967

INTRODUCTION

"MY JOY, I beg you, acquire the Spirit of Peace," said Fr. Seraphim to the monk, and at once he began to explain what it means to acquire the Spirit of Peace. "That means to bring oneself to such a state that our spirit will not be disturbed by anything. One must be like a dead man, or absolutely deaf and blind during any sorrow, calumny, accusation or persecution, which inevitably come to all those who wish to follow the saving path of Christ. For one must go through many sorrows to enter the Kingdom of Heaven. This is the way all righteous men were saved and inherited the Heavenly Kingdom. In comparison to this all the glory of this world is nothing. All the enjoyments of this world are not even a shadow of that which is prepared in the heavenly abodes for those who loved God: there, is eternal joy and triumph. So that our spirit will have freedom to uplift itself there and be nourished from sweetest conversation with the Lord, one must humble oneself with constant vigils, prayer and remembrance of the Lord.

"And I, humble Seraphim," said the Starets, "for this reason go through the Gospel daily. On Monday I read St. Matthew, from beginning to end; on Tuesday, St. Mark; on Wednesday, St. Luke; on Thursday, St. John; the other days I divide between the Acts of the Apostles and the Epistles of the Apostles. And I do not for a single day neglect to read the daily Epistle and Gospel, and also the readings about the saints. Through this not only my soul, but even my body rejoices and is vivified, because I converse with the Lord. I hold in my mind His Life and Suffering; and day and night I glorify and give thanks to my Redeemer for all His mercies that are shed upon mankind and upon me, the unworthy one."

Then, in indescribable joy, he uttered: "Here, I'll tell you about humble Seraphim! I took a special liking to the words of my Lord Jesus Christ: *In my*

The Krupenikov family portrait of St. Seraphim, painted in July, 1831.

Father's house are many mansions (John 14:2) (that is, for those who serve Him and glorify His holy name). On these words I, humble Seraphim, paused and wished to see these heavenly abodes, and I prayed my Lord Jesus Christ to show them to me; and the Lord did not deprive me, the humble one, of His mercy. He fulfilled my desire and request; and so I was transported to these heavenly abodes, only I do not know whether in the body or without the body, God knows—it is inconceivable. And about that joy and heavenly sweetness of which I partook there, it is impossible to tell you."

With these words Fr. Seraphim became silent.... He stooped his head, quietly patting his heart with his hand; his face began gradually to change and finally became so glowing that it was impossible to look at him. During this sacred silence he was as if contemplating something with humility.

Then Fr. Seraphim once more began to talk. "Oh, if only you could know," said the Starets to the monk, "what joy, what sweetness await the souls of the righteous in heaven, then you would be determined in this temporal life to endure any sorrow, persecution or calumny with gratitude. If this very cell of ours" (at this he pointed to his cell) "were full of worms, and if these worms were to eat our flesh throughout our whole temporal life, then with utmost desire we should consent to it, if only not to be deprived of that heavenly joy which God has prepared for those who love Him. There, there is no sickness, no sorrow, no lamentation; there is sweetness and rejoicing unutterable; there the righteous will shine like the sun. But if the holy Apostle Paul himself (II Cor. 12:2–4) could not explain that heavenly glory and joy, then what other human tongue could describe the beauty of the high dwelling in which the souls of the righteous shall dwell?"

At the conclusion of his talk the Starets spoke about how it is necessary to take attentive care of one's salvation—now, before the favorable time for this has passed.*

---

* From *The Diveyevo Chronicles* (St. Petersburg, 1903), in Russian.

A lithographic view of Sarov Monastery, with the churches of Sarov.
From left to right: the Church of St. John the Baptist, the Chapel over
St. Seraphim's relics, the Chapel of the Spring, the Church of All Saints,
and the Chapel over the relics of Saints Zosima and Sabbatius.

FOREWORD

by S. A. Nilus

*I*T CAME TO PASS, *that, while Apollos was at Corinth, Paul having passed through the upper coasts came to Ephesus and, finding certain disciples, he said unto them, Have ye received the Holy Spirit since ye believed? And they said unto him, We have not so much as heard whether there be any Holy Spirit. And he said unto them, Unto what then were ye baptized? And they said, Unto John's baptism. Paul said, John verily baptized with the baptism of repentance, saying unto the people, that they should believe on him which should come after him, that is, on Christ Jesus. When they heard this, they were baptized in the name of the Lord Jesus. And when Paul had laid his hands upon them, the Holy Spirit came on them; and they spake with tongues, and prophesied. And all the men were about twelve* (Acts 19:1–7).

And now, behold, I go bound in the spirit unto Jerusalem, not knowing the things that shall befall me there: save that the Holy Spirit witnesseth in every city, saying that bonds and afflictions await me (Acts 20:22–23).

And my speech and my preaching was not with enticing words of man's wisdom, but in demonstration of the Spirit and of power: that your faith should not stand in the wisdom of men, but in the power of God (I Cor. 2:4–5).

But God hath revealed it unto us by His Spirit: for the Spirit searcheth all things, yea, the deep things of God (I Cor. 2:10).

The natural man receiveth not the things of the Spirit of God: for they are foolishness unto him: neither can he know them, because they are spiritually discerned (I Cor. 2:14).

I was in the Spirit on the Lord's day, and heard behind me a great voice, as of a trumpet, saying, I am Alpha and Omega, the first and the last (Rev. 1:10–11).

Some months prior to the Imperial directive concerning the hastening of the work taking place in the Holy Synod on the canonization of the holy God-pleaser, Seraphim of Sarov, the Lord brought me again to Sarov and Diveyevo. Of the three contemporaries of Fr. Seraphim whom I had met on my first visit, I found only one still among the living, Elena Ivanovna Motovilova. Soon after my departure back in 1900, Mother Febronia departed to the habitations of the righteous. At Pascha two years later, Mother Evanthia followed after her.

These years had a powerful effect upon Elena Ivanovna: her figure had become stooped; her eyes, which not long before had been radiant and penetrating, had begun to grow dark. Seraphim no longer had need of earthly witnesses to his righteousness; he summoned them to himself to a place of eternal rest, to behold and share with him that incorrupt and eternal glory, that unfading glory, which the Lord from eternity has prepared for those who love Him, *where the choirs of the saints, O Lord, and of the righteous shall shine like the sun!* (Matt. 13:43, Dan. 12:3).

But clarity of mind and memory had not yet left the dear old woman. The past lived and flourished in her reminiscences, and time had not power over them....

At my request, with the approval of the Abbess, Elena Ivanovna gave me a whole parcel of papers which had been left by her late husband, Nicholas Alexandrovich. Everyone who is interested in the life of Fr. Seraphim should know his name, which is so closely linked with Batiushka's name and the Diveyevo Convent built by him. This man was misunderstood when he lived, and unappreciated when he died, Nevertheless he was, as he loved to call himself, "Seraphim's servant," and still remains so after his death. In his papers I managed to find such a treasure which in all fairness can only be called a great testimony of faith. This precious treasure, with the preservation of all of its characteristic style of the forties of the last century, at which time it was recorded, I wish to share with the Orthodox reader.*

---

* From "The Holy Spirit Clearly Resting upon Fr. Seraphim of Sarov in his Conversation on the Aim of the Christian Life with the Simbirsk Landowner and Judicial Counselor Nicholas Alexandrovich Motovilov," in *Greatness in Small Things* by S. A. Nilus (Moscow, 1903), in Russian.

I.

AN INVITATION

Verily, verily I say unto you; He who believes
in Me, the works that I do, he shall do also,
and greater works than these shall he do.
John 14:12

ONCE WHILE IN SAROV MONASTERY, writes Motovilov in his notes, soon after my healing in the beginning of the winter of 1831, on Tuesday at the end of November, I attended Vespers in the winter Cathedral of the Life-giving Spring, in my usual spot, as I would do later on, right across from the miracle-working icon of the Mother of God. At that time one of the sisters of the mill community of Diveyevo* approached me. Then I still had no awareness about this name and the existence of this community, separate from that of the other church community, also known as Diveyevo.

This sister asked me: "Are you that limping master whom our Batiushka Seraphim recently healed?"

I answered that yes, I was that very one.

"In that case," she said to me, "go to Batiushka. He ordered me to summon you to him. He is now in his cell in the Monastery and said that he will wait for you."

People who visited Sarov Monastery at least once during the life of the great Elder Seraphim, or perhaps only heard about him, can fully understand with what inexplicable joy my soul was filled at this unexpected invitation. Leaving the attendance of the Divine Service, I immediately ran to his cell. Batiushka Seraphim met me in the doorway of his vestibule and told me: "I

---

* At the Diveyevo Community, in the beginning of its existence, Fr. Seraphim instructed that a windmill be built so that the sisters, being poor, could provide for themselves from their own labor. From this mill they received the name of the mill sisters, and it was that part of the Convent where, according to the instructions of the Elder, only virgins (never married) were to be received.

was expecting your Godliness,* but wait for a short time until I finish talking with my orphans. I have much to say to you. Sit down here."

With these words he showed me a little ladder with steps, made evidently in order to close the stove pipes and placed opposite his stove, protruding into the vestibule, which was just as in other double cells built in Sarov Monastery. I sat down on the lowest step, but he told me: "No, sit a little higher."

I sat on the second, but he said to me: "No, your Godliness, sit down on the highest of the steps, please." And, having sat me down, he added: "Here, sit here and wait for me. When I have finished talking to my orphans I will come out to you."

The Elder conducted two sisters into his cell, one of whom was a maiden from the nobility, Helen Vasilievna, a sister of a Nizhny Novgorod landowner, Manturov. I was told about this in answer to my inquiry by those who remained with me in the waiting room.

I sat for a long time waiting for the great Elder to open the door for me. I think that I sat like this for two hours. Then from the door next to the entrance of the cell, the cell-attendant of Fr. Seraphim, Paul, came out and in spite of my refusal convinced me to visit his cell and began to give me various instructions in spiritual life, which, in actuality prompted by the evil one, had the purpose of weakening my love and faith in the merits before God of the great Elder Seraphim.

I became sad, and with sorrow said to him: "It was silly of me, Fr. Paul, that, listening to your enticements, I entered your cell. Fr. Abbot Niphon is a great slave of God, but even he is not the purpose for my visit to Sarov Monastery. For I have come only because of Fr. Seraphim, about whom I think that even in ancient times there were few such holy God-pleasers, gifted with the power of Elias and Moses. Who are you that you are forcing upon me your instructions when, as I suspect, you yourself do not know the path to God well enough? Forgive me. I regret that I listened to you and entered your cell."

---

* Lit., "Your God-lovingness," corresponding to the English idioms "Your Worship," "Your Excellency," etc.

With this I left his cell and sat down again on the top plank of the ladder in the vestibule of the Elder's cell. Later I heard from the same Fr. Paul that the Elder severely reprimanded him for that, saying: "It is not your business to talk to them who thirst for the words of humble Seraphim and who deliberately travel to see him at Sarov. I, the unworthy one, do not tell them anything of myself, but that which is pleasing to the Lord to reveal to me for edification of others. Do not meddle in what is not your own business. Know yourself, and do not dare to teach anyone. God did not give you this gift—for it is given to people not in vain, but for service before our Lord God and for His special mercy and His divine care of people, according to His holy Providence." I am entering these words here as a reminder and instruction, treasuring even the briefest talks and subtlest character traits of the great Elder Seraphim.

After the Elder had conversed for about two hours with his orphans, the door opened and Batiushka Seraphim, having parted with the sisters, said to me: "I kept you, your Godliness, for a long time. Do not hold it against me. These little orphans of mine were in need of many things; so I, the unworthy one, was consoling them. Please enter my cell."

In this cell, his monastery cell, he talked with me on various subjects related to the salvation of my soul and secular life, and invited me with Fr. Gurias, the Sarov guestmaster, to come to see him the next day after the early Liturgy in his near hermitage.

2.

THE WILL OF THE LORD

I SPOKE WITH FR. GURIAS about Fr. Seraphim the entire night, almost not having slept at all from joy, and the next day we headed for Batiushka Seraphim in his near hermitage, not even having had anything to drink nor having eaten; and we spent the entire day until late at night at the door of his near hermitage, again not having had anything to drink or anything to eat. Thousands of people came to the great Elder, and after having stood awhile in his vestibule they all departed, not having received his blessing. About seven or eight people remained with us to await the end of the day and the departure of Batiushka Seraphim from his hermitage. In that group, as I now recall, was the wife of a Balakhin treasurer, from the district city Balakhin of the Nizhegorod Province, and a certain woman pilgrim who was busy petitioning for the opening of the holy relics of St. Paphnutius, which apparently lay incorrupt in Balakhin. They decided to wait with us for the opening of the doors of the great Elder. Finally, they became disconcerted in spirit, and, as it was by then already late evening, even Fr. Gurias was very disconcerted and said to me: "It is already dark, Batiushka; the horse is hungry, and the boy coachman wants to eat. It may be that if we go any later, wild animals might attack us."*

But I said: "No, Batiushka Gurias, you should travel back alone if you fear that; but though the beasts may tear me to pieces here, I will not go away from the doors of Batiushka Seraphim. Even if I happen to die from hunger before them, nevertheless I will remain to await him until he opens the doors of his holy cell."

And Batiushka Seraphim just a little later did, in fact, open the doors of his cell and, turning to me, said:

"Your Godliness, I summoned you, but do not hold it against me that I did not open the doors for the entire day. It is now Wednesday, and I am keeping silence. Tomorrow you would be welcome; I will be glad to converse with you heart-to-heart. But do not deign to visit me so early since, not having eaten all day, you have grown quite weak. Therefore, after the late Liturgy, having fortified yourself with sufficient food, visit me with Fr. Gurias. Now go and strengthen yourself with some food—you have grown weak."

And he began to bless us, starting with me, and said to Fr. Gurias: "Thus, friend, my joy, visit me tomorrow with his lordship at my nearer plot of ground; come to me there. But now go in peace. Good-bye, your Godliness."

With these words Batiushka again shut himself up.

---

* One would have to know the virgin Sarov forest, which surrounded the Sarov Monastery for tens of thousands of acres, in order to understand the natural fear of Fr. Gurias.

Above: St. Seraphim's far hermitage; below: his near hermitage.

No words can express the joy which I felt in my heart. I swam in bliss. In spite of the long-suffering of an entire day, the thought that I, although at the very end of the day, had been vouchsafed nonetheless not only to behold the face of Fr. Seraphim, but even to hear the greeting of his divinely inspired words, consoled me greatly. Yea, I was on the height of blessedness, which cannot be depicted by any earthly likeness. And in spite of the fact that I had neither drunk nor eaten the entire day, I had become so filled that it was as if I had eaten to satiety and had drunk to mental rapture. I speak the truth, although it may be that for certain people—who have not experienced in actual fact what sweetness, satiety and ecstasy mean, with which a man is imbued during the time of inspiration from the Spirit of God—my words may seem exaggerated and my narrative too ecstatic. But I attest with my Orthodox Christian conscience that there isn't any exaggeration here and that all that has now been said by me is not only the very truth, but even an extremely feeble representation of that which I actually felt in my heart.

But who shall give me words that I might, although briefly, although in part, express what my soul sensed on the following day?

3.

THE AIM OF THE CHRISTIAN LIFE

IT WAS THURSDAY. The day was gloomy. The snow lay eight inches deep on the ground; and dry, crisp snowflakes were falling thickly from the sky when Batiushka Seraphim began his conversation with me in a field adjoining his hermitage nearby, opposite the river Sarovka, at the foot of the hill which slopes down to the river bank. He sat me on a stump of a tree which he had just felled, and he himself squatted opposite me.

"The Lord has revealed to me," said the great Elder, "that in your childhood you had a great desire to know the aim of our Christian life, and that you continually asked many great spiritual persons about it...."

I must say here that from the age of twelve this thought had constantly troubled me. I had, in fact, approached many clergy about it; but their answers had not satisfied me. This was not known to the Elder.

"But no one," continued Fr. Seraphim, "has given you a precise answer. They have said to you: 'Go to church, pray to God, do the commandments of God, do good—that is the aim of the Christian life.' Some were even indignant with you for being occupied with curiosity displeasing to God and said to you: 'Do not seek things which are beyond you.' But they did not speak as they should. And now poor Seraphim will explain to you in what this aim really consists.

"Prayer, fasting, vigil and all other Christian practices, however good they may be in themselves, do not constitute the aim of our Christian life, although they serve as the indispensable means of reaching this end. The true aim of our Christian life consists in the acquisition of the HOLY SPIRIT OF GOD. As for fasts, and vigils, and prayer, and almsgiving, and every good deed done for Christ's sake, they are only the means of acquiring the Holy Spirit of God. But mark, my dear, only the good deed done for Christ's sake brings us the fruits of the Holy Spirit. All that is not done for Christ's sake, even though it be good, brings neither reward in the future life nor the grace of God in this life. That is why our Lord Jesus Christ said: *He who gathers not with Me scatters* (Luke 11:23). A good deed can be called anything but gathering, since even though it is not done for Christ's sake, yet it is good. Scripture says: *In every nation he who fears God and works righteousness is acceptable to Him* (Acts 10:35).

"As we see from the sacred narrative, *he who worketh righteousness* is so pleasing to God that the angel of the Lord appeared at the hour of prayer to Cornelius, the God-fearing and righteous centurion, and said: 'Send to Joppa to Simon the Tanner; there shalt thou find Peter and he will tell thee the words of eternal life, whereby thou shalt be saved and all thy house.'* Thus the Lord uses all His divine means to give such a man in return for his good works the opportunity not to lose his reward in the future life. But to this end we must begin with a right faith in our Lord Jesus Christ, the Son of God, Who came into the world to save sinners and Who, through our acquiring for ourselves the grace of the Holy Spirit, brings into our hearts the Kingdom of God and opens the way for us to win the blessings of the future

---

* Cf. Acts 10:5.

life. But the acceptability to God of good deeds not done for Christ's sake is limited to this: the Creator gives the means to make them living (cf. Heb. 6:1). It rests with man to make them living or not. That is why the Lord said to the Jews: *If you had been blind, you would have had no sin. But now you say, We see, and your sin remains on you* (John 9:4). If a man like Cornelius enjoys the favor of God for his deeds, though not done for Christ's sake, and then believes in His Son, such deeds will be imputed to him as done for Christ's sake merely for faith in Him. But in the opposite event a man has no right to complain that his good has been of no use. It never is of any use, except when it is done for Christ's sake, since good done for Him not only merits a crown of righteousness in the world to come, but also in this present life fills us with the grace of the Holy Spirit; and moreover, as it is said: *God gives not the Holy Spirit by measure. The Father loves the Son, and has given all things into His hand* (John 3:34–35).

"That's it, your Godliness. In acquiring the Spirit of God consists the true aim of our Christian life, while prayer, fasting, almsgiving and other good works* done for Christ's sake are merely means for acquiring the Spirit of God."

"What do you mean by acquiring?" I asked Batiushka Seraphim. "Somehow I don't understand that."

"Acquiring is the same as obtaining," he replied to me. "You understand, of course, what acquiring money means. Acquiring the Spirit of God is exactly the same. You know well what it means in a worldly sense, your Godliness, to acquire. The aim in life of ordinary worldly people is to acquire or make money, and for the nobility it is in addition to receive honors, distinctions and other rewards for their services to the government. The acquisition of God's Spirit is also capital, but grace-giving and eternal; and it is obtained in very similar ways, almost the same ways as monetary, social and temporal capital.

"God the Word, the God-Man, our Lord Jesus Christ, compares our life with a market, and the work of our life on earth He calls trading, and says to us all: *Trade till I come* (Luke 19:13), *redeeming the time, because the days*

---

* "Good works." It is one compound word in Russian and may also be translated "virtues."

are evil (Eph. 5:16), that is to say, make the most of your time for getting heavenly blessings through earthly goods. Earthly goods are good works done for Christ's sake and conferring on us the grace of the All-Holy Spirit.

"In the parable of the wise and foolish virgins, when the foolish ones lacked oil, it was said: 'Go and buy in the market.' But when they had bought, the door of the bridechamber was already shut and they could not get in. Some say that the lack of oil in the lamps of the foolish virgins means a lack of good deeds in their lifetime. Such an interpretation is not quite correct. Why should they be lacking in good deeds if they are called virgins, even though foolish ones? Virginity is the supreme virtue, an angelic state, and it could take the place of all other good works.

"I, the humble one, think that what they were lacking was the grace of the All-Holy Spirit of God. These virgins practiced the virtues, but in their spiritual ignorance they supposed that the Christian life consisted merely in doing good works. By doing a good deed they thought they were doing the work of God, but they little cared whether they acquired thereby the grace of God's Spirit. Such ways of life based merely on doing good without carefully testing whether they bring the grace of the Spirit of God, are mentioned in the patristic books: *There is another way which appears as good at the beginning, but it ends at the bottom of hell* (Prov. 16:25).

"Anthony the Great in his letters to monks says of such virgins: 'Many monks and virgins have no idea of the different kinds of wills which act in man, and they do not know that we are influenced by three wills: the first is God's all-perfect and all-saving will; the second is our human will which, if not destructive, yet neither is it saving; and the third will is the devil's will—wholly destructive.' And this third will of the enemy teaches man either not to do any good deeds, or to do them out of vainglory, or for some other good, but not for Christ's sake. The second, our own will, teaches us to do everything to flatter our passions, or else it teaches us to do good for the sake of good and not to care for the grace which is acquired by it. But the first, God's all-saving will, consists in doing good solely to acquire the Holy Spirit as an eternal, inexhaustible treasure which cannot be rightly valued. The acquisition of the Holy Spirit is, so to say, the oil which the foolish virgins lacked. They were called foolish just because they had forgotten the necessary fruit of virtue, the grace of the Holy Spirit, without which no one is or can be saved, for: 'Every soul is quickened by the Holy Spirit and exalted by purity and mystically illumined by the Trinal Unity' (Hymn of Degrees, tone four, first antiphon). The Holy Spirit Himself takes up His abode in our souls, and this very settling into our souls of His Omnipotence and His abiding with our spirit of His Trinal Unity grants to us every possible means of acquiring the Holy Spirit which prepares in our soul and body a throne for God by means of His all-creating indwelling with our spirit, according to the unlying Word of God: *I will dwell in them and walk in them; and I will be to them a God and they shall be My people* (II Cor. 6:16).

"This is the oil in the lamps of the wise virgins which could burn long and brightly; and these virgins with their burning lamps were able to meet the Bridegroom, Who came at midnight, and could enter the bridechamber of joy with Him. But the foolish ones, though they went to market to buy some oil when they saw their lamps going out, were unable to return in time, for the door was already shut. The market is our life; the door of the bridechamber which was shut and which barred the way to the Bridegroom is human death; the wise and foolish virgins are Christian souls; the oil is not good deeds but the grace of the All-Holy Spirit of God which is obtained through them and which changes souls from one state to another—that is, from corruption to incorruption, from spiritual death to spiritual life, from darkness to light, from the stable of our being (where the passions are tied up like dumb animals and wild beasts) into a temple of the Divinity, into the shining bridechamber of eternal joy in Christ Jesus our Lord, the Creator and Redeemer and eternal Bridegroom of our souls.

"How great is God's compassion on our misery, that is to say, our inattention to His care for us, when God says: *Behold, I stand at the door and knock* (Rev. 3:20), meaning by 'door' the course of our life which has not yet been closed by death! Oh, how I wish, your Godliness, that in this life you may always be in the Spirit of God! 'In whatsoever I find you, in that will I judge you,' says the Lord.*

---

* St. Justin (Dialogue 47) records this "unwritten saying" of Christ.

82

"Woe, great woe to us if He finds us overcharged with the cares and sorrows of this life! For who will be able to bear His anger, who will withstand the wrath of His countenance? That is why it has been said: *Watch and pray, lest you enter into temptation* (Mark 14:38), that is, lest you be deprived of the Spirit of God, for watching and prayer brings us His grace.

"Of course, every good deed done for Christ's sake gives us the grace of the Holy Spirit, but prayer gives it to us most of all, for it is always at hand, so to speak, as an instrument for acquiring the grace of the Spirit. For instance, you would like to go to church, but there is no church or the service is over; you would like to give alms to a beggar, but there isn't one, or you have nothing to give; you would like to preserve your virginity,* but you have not the strength to do so because of your temperament, or because of the violence of the wiles of the enemy which on account of your human weakness you cannot withstand; you would like to do some other good deed for Christ's sake, but either you have not the strength or the opportunity is lacking. This certainly does not apply to prayer. Prayer is always possible for everyone, rich and poor, noble and humble, strong and weak, healthy and sick, righteous and sinful.

"You may judge how great the power of prayer is even in a sinful person, when it is offered wholeheartedly, by the following example from Holy Tradition.** When at the request of a desperate mother who had been deprived by death of her only son, a harlot whom she chanced to meet, still unclean from her last sin, and who was touched by the mother's deep sorrow, cried to the Lord: 'Not for the sake of a wretched sinner like me, but for the sake of the tears of a mother sorrowing for her son and firmly trusting in Thy

---

* That is, you would like to remain unmarried.

** The Life of St. Benedict (commemorated on the 14th of March) records the following: "A certain farmer, carrying in his arms the lifeless body of his son, came to see the saint, entreating him to resurrect his son. The saint knelt down with the brothers in prayer and said to God: 'O Lord, do not consider my sins but the faith of this man who is asking to see his son alive again, and restore to this body his soul.' Hardly had the saint finished his prayer when the child's whole body began once more to throb with life. The saint took the little boy by the hand and gave him back to his father alive and well."

See also St. Gregory the Great, *Dialogues,* (New York: Fathers of the Church, Inc., 1959), pp. 100–101.

lovingkindness and Thy almighty power, Christ God, raise up her son, O Lord!' And the Lord raised him up.

"You see, your Godliness! Great is the power of prayer, and it brings most of all the Spirit of God and is most easily practiced by everyone. We shall be blessed if the Lord God finds us watchful and filled with the gifts of His Holy Spirit. Then we may boldly hope *to be caught up ... in the clouds to meet the Lord in the air* (I Thess. 4:17) *Who is coming with great power and glory* (Mark 13:26) *to judge the living and the dead* (I Peter 4:5) and *to reward every man according to his works* (Matt. 16:27).

"Your Godliness deigns to think it a great happiness to talk to poor Seraphim, believing that even he is not bereft of the grace of the Lord. What then shall we say of the Lord Himself, the never-failing source of every blessing, both heavenly and earthly? Truly in prayer we are granted to converse with Him, our all-gracious and life-giving God and Savior Himself. But even here we must pray only until God the Holy Spirit descends on us in measures of His heavenly grace known to Him. And when He deigns to visit us, we must stop praying. Why should we then pray to Him, 'Come and abide in us and cleanse us from all impurity and save our souls, O Good One,' when He has already come to us to save us who trust in Him, and truly call on His holy name, hungering and thirsting for His coming, that humbly we may receive Him, the Comforter, in the mansions of our souls?

"I will explain this to your Godliness by an example. Imagine that you have invited me to pay you a visit and at your invitation I come to have a talk with you. But you continue to invite me, saying: 'Come in, please. Do come in!' Then I should be obliged to think: 'What is the matter with him? Is he out of his mind?' So it is with regard to our Lord God the Holy Spirit. That is why it is said: *Be still and realize that I am God; I shall be exalted among the heathen, I shall be exalted in the earth* (Ps. 45:10). That is, I shall appear and shall continue to appear to everyone who believes in Me and calls upon Me; and I shall converse with him as once I conversed with Adam in Paradise, with Abraham and Jacob and other servants of Mine, with Moses and Job, and those like them.

"Many explain that this stillness refers only to worldly matters; in other words, that during prayerful converse with God you must 'be still' with re-

Lithograph of St. Seraphim from Diveyevo, 1880,
based on one printed during his lifetime.

gard to worldly affairs. But I will tell you in the name of God that not only is it necessary to be dead* to them at prayer, but when by the omnipotent power of faith and prayer our Lord God the Holy Spirit condescends to visit us, and comes to us in the plenitude of His unutterable goodness, we must be dead to prayer, too.

"The soul speaks and converses during prayer, but at the descent of the Holy Spirit we must remain in complete silence in order to hear clearly and intelligibly all the words of eternal life which He will then deign to communicate. Complete sobriety of soul and spirit and chaste purity of body is required at the same time. The same demands were made at Mount Horeb, when the Israelites were told not even to touch their wives for three days before the appearance of God on Mount Sinai. For our God is a fire which consumes everything unclean, and no one who is defiled in flesh or spirit can enter into communion with Him."

4.

THE ACQUISITION OF GRACE

YES, FATHER, but what about other good deeds done for Christ's sake in order to acquire the grace of the Holy Spirit? You have only been speaking of prayer."

"Acquire the grace of the Holy Spirit also by practicing all the other virtues for Christ's sake. Trade spiritually with them; trade with those which give you the greatest profit. Accumulate capital from the superabundance of God's grace; deposit it in God's eternal bank which will bring you immaterial interest, not four or six percent, but one hundred percent for one spiritual rouble, and even infinitely more than that. For example, if prayer and watching gives you more of God's grace, watch and pray; if fasting gives you much of the Spirit of God, fast; if almsgiving gives you more, give alms. Weigh every virtue done for Christ's sake in this manner.

---

* Lit. "be still."

"Now, I will tell you about myself, poor Seraphim. I come of a merchant family in Kursk. So when I was not yet in the monastery we used to trade with goods which brought us the greatest profit. Act like that, my dear. And just as in business the main point is not merely to trade, but to get just as much profit as possible, so in the business of the Christian life the main point is not merely to pray or to do some other good deed. Though the Apostle says: *Pray without ceasing* (I Thess. 5:17), yet, as you remember, he adds: *I would rather speak five words with my understanding than ten thousand words in an unknown tongue* (I Cor. 14:13). And the Lord says: *Not everyone who says to Me: Lord, Lord,* shall be saved, *but he who does the will of My Father* (Matt. 7:21), that is, he who does the work of God and, moreover, does it with reverence, for *cursed is he who does the work of God negligently* (Jer. 48:10). And the work of God is: *Believe in God and in Him Whom He has sent,* Jesus Christ (John 14:1; 6:29). If we understand the commandments of Christ and of the Apostles aright, our business as Christians consists not in increasing the number of our good deeds, which are only the means of furthering the purpose of our Christian life, but in deriving from them the utmost profit, that is, in acquiring the most abundant gifts of the Holy Spirit.

"How I wish, your Godliness, that you yourself may acquire this inexhaustible source of divine grace, and may always ask yourself: 'Am I in the Spirit of God or not?' And if you are in the Spirit, blessed be God!—there is nothing to grieve about. You are ready to appear before the dread judgment of Christ immediately. For 'In whatsoever I find you, in that will I judge you.' But if we are not in the Spirit, we must discover why and for what reason our Lord God the Holy Spirit has willed to abandon us; we must seek Him again through His goodness. And we must attack the enemies that drive us away from Him until even their dust is no more, as has been said by the Prophet David: *I shall pursue my enemies and overtake them; and I shall not turn back until they are destroyed. I shall harass them, and they will not be able to stand; they will fall under my feet* (Ps. 17:31–38).

"That's it, my dear. That is how you must spiritually trade in virtue. Distribute the Holy Spirit's gifts of grace to those in need of them, just as a lighted candle burning with earthly fire shines itself and lights other candles for the illumining of all in other places, without diminishing its own light.

And if it is so with regard to earthly fire, what shall we say about the fire of the grace of the All-Holy Spirit of God? For earthly riches when distributed are diminished, yet the more the heavenly riches of God's grace are distributed, the more they increase in him who distributes them. Thus the Lord Himself was pleased to say to the Samaritan woman: *Whoever drinks of this water will thirst again, but whoever drinks of the water that I shall give him will never thirst; but the water that I shall give him will be in him a well of water springing up into eternal life* (John 4:13–14)."

5.

THE PRESENCE OF THE HOLY SPIRIT IN HISTORY

FATHER," said I, "you speak all the time of the acquisition of the grace of the Holy Spirit as the aim of the Christian life. But how and where can I see it? Good deeds are visible, but can the Holy Spirit be seen? How am I to know whether He is with me or not?"

"At the present time," the Elder replied, "owing to our almost universal coldness to our holy faith in our Lord Jesus Christ, and to our inattention to the working of His Divine Providence in us, and the communion of man with God, we have gone so far that, one may say, we have almost abandoned the true Christian life. The testimonies of Holy Scripture now seem strange to us when, for instance, by the lips of Moses the Holy Spirit says: 'And Adam saw the Lord walking in paradise' (cf. Gen. 3:10), or when we read the words of the Apostle Paul: 'We went to Achaia, and the Spirit of God went not with us; we returned to Macedonia, and the Spirit of God came with us.'* More than once in other passages of Holy Scripture the appearance of God to men is mentioned.

"That is why some people say: 'These passages are incomprehensible. Is it really possible for people to see God so openly?' But there is nothing incomprehensible here. This failure to understand has come about because we have departed from the simplicity of the original Christian knowledge. Under

---

* In the Acts of the Apostles (16:6–7) this text reads: *When they had gone throughout Phrygia and the region of Galatia, and were forbidden of the Holy Spirit to preach the word in Asia, after they were come to Mysia, they assayed to go into Bithynia: but the Spirit suffered them not.*

the pretext of education, we have reached such a darkness of ignorance that what the ancients understood so clearly seems to us almost inconceivable. Even in ordinary conversation, the idea of God's appearance among men did not seem strange to them. Thus, when his friends rebuked him for blaspheming God, Job answered them: 'How can that be when I feel the Spirit of God in my nostrils?' (cf. Job 27:3). That is, how can I blaspheme God when the Holy Spirit abides with me? If I had blasphemed God, the Holy Spirit would have withdrawn from me; but lo, I feel His breath in my nostrils.

"In exactly the same way it is said of Abraham and Jacob that they saw the Lord and conversed with Him, and that Jacob even wrestled with Him. Moses and all the people with him saw God when he was granted to receive from God the tables of the law on Mount Sinai. A pillar of cloud and a pillar of fire, or in other words, the evident grace of the Holy Spirit, served as guides to the people of God in the desert. People saw God and the grace of His Holy Spirit not in sleep or in dreams, or in the excitement of a disordered imagination, but truly and openly.

"We have become so inattentive to the work of salvation that we misinterpret many other words in Holy Scripture as well, all because we do not seek the grace of God and in the pride of our minds do not allow it to dwell in our souls. That is why we are without true enlightenment from the Lord, which He sends into the hearts of men who hunger and thirst wholeheartedly for God's righteousness.

"Many explain that when it says in the Bible: 'God breathed the breath of life into the face of Adam the first-created, who was created by Him from the dust of the ground' (cf. Gen. 2:7), it must mean that until then there was neither human soul nor spirit in Adam, but only the flesh created from the dust of the ground. This interpretation is wrong, for the Lord created Adam from the dust of the ground with the constitution which the holy Batiushka Apostle Paul describes: *May your spirit and soul and body be preserved blameless at the coming of our Lord Jesus Christ* (I Thess. 5:23). And all these three parts of our nature were created from the dust of the ground; Adam was not created dead, but an active living being like all the other animate creatures of God living on earth. The point is that if the Lord God had not then breathed into his face this breath of life (that is, the grace of our Lord God the Holy

Spirit, Who proceeds from the Father and rests in the Son and is sent into the world for the Son's sake), Adam, however perfect he had been created and superior to all the other creatures of God as the crown of creation on earth, nevertheless would have been without the Holy Spirit within himself, like unto the other creatures, although he possessed flesh, soul and spirit. But when the Lord God breathed into Adam's face the breath of life, then, according to Moses' expression, *Adam became a living soul* (Gen. 2:7), that is, completely and in every way like God, and, like Him, forever immortal. Adam was immune to the action of the elements to such a degree that water could not drown him, fire could not burn him, the earth could not swallow him in its abysses, and the air could not harm him by any kind of action whatever. Everything was subject to him as the beloved of God, as the king and lord of creation; and everything looked up to him, as the perfect crown of God's creatures. Adam was made so wise by this breath of life which was breathed into his face from the creative lips of God, the Creator and Ruler of all, that there never has been a man on earth wiser or more intelligent than he, and it is hardly likely that there ever will be. When the Lord commanded him to give names to all the creatures, he gave every creature a name which completely expressed all the qualities, powers and properties given it by God at its creation.

"Owing to this very gift of the supernatural grace of God which was infused into him by the breath of life, Adam could see and understand the Lord walking in paradise and comprehend His words, and the conversation of the holy angels, and the language of all the beasts, birds and reptiles and all that is now hidden from us fallen and sinful creatures, but was so clear to Adam before his fall. To Eve also the Lord God gave the same wisdom, strength and unlimited power, and all the other good and holy qualities. And He created her not from the dust of the ground, but from Adam's rib in the Eden of delight, in the Paradise which He had planted in the midst of the earth.

"In order that they might always easily maintain within themselves the immortal, divine* and perfect properties of this breath of life, God planted in the midst of the garden the tree of life and endowed its fruits with all the es-

---

* Lit. "God-gracious" or "Divine-grace-given."

sence and fullness of His divine breath. If they had not sinned, Adam and Eve themselves, as well as all their posterity, could have always eaten of the fruit of the tree of life and so would have eternally maintained the quickening power of divine grace.

"They also could have maintained to all eternity the full powers of their body, soul and spirit in a state of immortality and everlasting youth, and they could have continued in this immortal and blessed state of theirs forever. At the present time, however, it is difficult for us even to imagine such grace.

"But when through the tasting of the tree of the knowledge of good and evil—which was premature and contrary to the commandment of God—they learned the difference between good and evil and were subjected to all the afflictions which followed the transgression of the commandment of God; then they lost this priceless gift of the grace of the Spirit of God, so that until the actual coming into the world of the God-Man Jesus Christ, *The Spirit of God was not yet* in the world *because Jesus was not yet glorified* (John 7:39).

"However, that does not mean that the Spirit of God was not in the world at all, but His presence was not so apparent* as in Adam or in us Orthodox Christians. It manifested only externally; yet the signs of His presence in the world were known to mankind. Thus, for instance, many mysteries in connection with the future salvation of the human race were revealed to Adam as well as to Eve after the fall. And for Cain, in spite of his impiety and his transgression, it was easy to understand the voice which held gracious and divine though convicting converse with him. Noah conversed with God. Abraham saw God and His days and was glad (cf. John 8:56). The grace of the Holy Spirit acting externally was also reflected in all the Old Testament prophets and saints of Israel. The Hebrews afterwards established special prophetic schools where the sons of the prophets were taught to discern the signs of the manifestation of God or angels, and to distinguish the operations of the Holy Spirit from the ordinary natural phenomena of our graceless earthly life. Symeon who held God in his arms, Christ's grandparents, Joachim and

---

* Lit. "His abiding (stay, sojourn, dwelling, residence) was not so full-measured."

91

Anna, and countless other servants of God continually had quite openly various divine apparitions, voices and revelations which were justified* by evident miraculous events. Though not with the same power as in the people of God, nevertheless the presence of the Spirit of God also acted in the pagans who did not know the true God, because even among them God found for Himself chosen people. Such, for instance, were the virgin-prophetesses called Sibyls who vowed virginity to an unknown God, but still to God the Creator of the universe, the all-powerful ruler of the world, as He was conceived of by the pagans. Though the pagan philosophers also wandered in the darkness of ignorance of God, yet they sought the truth which is beloved by God; and on account of this God-pleasing seeking, they could partake of the Spirit of God, for it is said that the nations who do not know God practice by nature the demands of the law and do what is pleasing to God (cf. Rom. 2:14). The Lord so praises truth that He says of it Himself by the Holy Spirit: *Truth is sprung up out of the earth, and righteousness hath looked down from heaven* (Ps. 84:11).

"So you see, your Godliness, both in the holy Hebrew people, a people beloved by God, and in the pagans who did not know God, there was preserved a knowledge of God—that is, my dear, a clear and rational comprehension of how our Lord God the Holy Spirit acts in man, and by means of what inner and outer feelings one can be sure that this is really the action of our Lord God the Holy Spirit and not a delusion of the enemy. That is how it was from Adam's fall until the coming in the flesh of our Lord Jesus Christ into the world.

"Without this perceptible realization of the actions of the Holy Spirit, your godliness, which had always been preserved in human nature, men could not have possibly known for certain whether the fruit of the seed of the woman who had been promised to Adam and Eve had come into the world to bruise the serpent's head (cf. Gen. 3:15).

"At last the Holy Spirit foretold to St. Symeon, who was then in his 65th year, the mystery of the virginal conception and birth of Christ from the Most Pure Ever-Virgin Mary. Afterwards, having lived by the grace of the

---

* Or, "were proved true."

All-Holy Spirit of God for three hundred years, in the 365th year of his life he said openly in the temple of the Lord that he knew for certain* through the gift of the Holy Spirit that this was that very Christ, the Savior of the world, Whose supernatural conception and birth from the Holy Spirit had been foretold to him by an angel three hundred years previously.

"And there was also St. Anna, a prophetess, the daughter of Phanuel, who from her widowhood had served the Lord God in the temple of God for eighty years and who was known to be a righteous widow, a chaste servant of God, from the special gifts of grace which she had received. She too announced that He was actually the Messiah Who had been promised to the world, the true Christ, God and Man, the King of Israel, Who had come to save Adam and mankind.

"But when our Lord Jesus Christ condescended to accomplish the whole work of salvation, after His resurrection He breathed on the Apostles, restored the breath of life lost by Adam, and gave them the same grace of the All-Holy Spirit of God as Adam had enjoyed. But that was not all. He also told them that it was expedient for them that He should go to the Father, for if He did not go, the Spirit of God would not come into the world. But if He, the Christ, went to the Father, He would send Him into the world, and He, the Comforter, would guide them and all who followed their teaching into all truth and would remind them of all that He had said to them when He was still in the world. What was then promised was *grace upon grace* (John 1:16).

"Then on the day of Pentecost He solemnly sent down to them in a tempestuous wind the Holy Spirit in the form of tongues of fire which alighted on each of them and entered within them and filled them with the fiery strength of divine grace which breathes bedewingly and acts gladdeningly in souls which partake of its power and operations (cf. Acts 2:1–4). And this same fire-infusing grace of the Holy Spirit which was given to us all, the faithful of Christ, in the Sacrament of Holy Baptism, is sealed by the Sacrament of Chrismation on the chief parts of our body as appointed by the Holy Church, the eternal keeper of this grace. It is said: 'The seal of the Gift of the Holy Spirit.' On what do we put our seal, your Godliness, if not on vessels

---

* Knew for certain. Lit. "palpably recognized" or "perceptibly realized."

containing some very precious treasure? But what on earth can be higher and what can be more precious than the gifts of the Holy Spirit which are sent down to us from above in the Sacrament of Holy Baptism? This baptismal grace is so great and so indispensable, so vital for man, that even a heretic is not deprived of it until his very death; that is, until the end of the period appointed on high by the Providence of God as a lifelong test of man on earth, in order to see what he will be able to achieve (during this period given to him by God) by means of the power of grace granted him from on high.

"And if we were never to sin after our baptism, we should remain forever saints of God—holy, blameless, and free from all impurity of body and spirit. But the trouble is that we increase in stature, but do not increase in grace and in the knowledge of God, as our Lord Jesus Christ increased; but on the contrary, we gradually become more and more depraved and lose the grace of the All-Holy Spirit of God and become sinful in various degrees, and most sinful people. But if a man is stirred by the wisdom of God, which seeks our salvation and embraces everything, and he is resolved for its sake to devote the early hours to God and to watch in order to find His eternal salvation,* then, in obedience to its voice, he must hasten to offer true repentance for all his sins and must practice the virtues which are opposite to the sins committed. Then through the virtues practiced for Christ's sake, he will acquire the Holy Spirit, Who acts within us and establishes in us the Kingdom of God. The word of God does not say in vain: *The Kingdom of God is within you* (Luke 17:21), and *it suffers violence, and the violent take it by force*** (Matt. 11:12). This means the people who, in spite of the bonds of sin which fetter them and hinder them (by constraint and by inciting them to new sins), come to Him, our Savior, with perfect repentance for tormenting Him, who despise all the strength of the fetters of sin and force themselves to break their bonds—such people at last actually appear before the face of God made whiter than snow by His grace. *Come, says the Lord: Though your sins be as scarlet, I will make them whiter than snow* (Is. 1:18).

---

* Cf. Wisdom 7:27; 6:14–20.
** Lit, "The Kingdom of Heaven is forced, and the forceful seize it." Cf. Luke 16:16: "Everyone forces himself into it."

"Such people were once seen by the holy seer of mysteries John the Theologian *clothed in white robes* (that is, in robes of justification) and *palms in their hands* (as a sign of victory), and they were singing to God a wonderful song: Alleluia. And no one could imitate the beauty of their song. Of them an angel of God said: *These are they who have come out of great tribulation and have washed their robes, and have made them white in the blood of the Lamb* (Rev. 7:9–14). They were washed with their sufferings and made white in the Communion of the immaculate and life-giving Mysteries of the Body and Blood of the most pure spotless Lamb—Christ—Who was slain before all ages by His own will for the salvation of the world, and Who is continually being slain and divided until now, but is never exhausted. Through the Holy Mysteries we are granted our eternal and unfailing salvation as a viaticum to eternal life, as an acceptable answer at His dread judgment and a precious substitute beyond our comprehension for that fruit of the tree of life, of which the enemy of mankind, Lucifer, who fell from heaven, would have liked to deprive our human race. Though the enemy and devil seduced Eve, and Adam fell with her, yet the Lord not only granted them in the fruit of the seed of a woman a Redeemer Who trampled down death by death; but also granted us all in the woman, the Ever-Virgin Mary Mother of God—who crushes the head of the serpent in herself and in all the human race—a constant mediatress with her Son and our God, and a blameless, invincible intercessor even for the most desperate sinners. That is why the Mother of God is called the 'Scourge of Demons,' for it is not possible for a devil to destroy a man so long as the man himself does not refrain from running to the help of the Mother of God.

6.

GRACE IS LIGHT

AND I, POOR SERAPHIM, must further explain, your Godliness, the difference between the operations of the Holy Spirit Who dwells mystically in the hearts of those who believe in our Lord, God and Savior Jesus Christ and the operations of the darkness of sin which, at the suggestion and

The repose of St. Seraphim before the icon of
the Mother of God, "Joy of All Joys."

instigation of the devil, act predatorily in us. The Spirit of God reminds us of the words of our Lord Jesus Christ and acts invisibly with Him, always triumphantly, gladdening our hearts and guiding our steps in the way of peace; while the false, diabolical spirit reasons in the opposite way to Christ, and its actions in us are rebellious, stubborn, and full of the lust of the flesh, the lust of the eyes and the pride of life.

"*Whoever lives and believes in Me shall not die forever* (John 11:26). He who has the grace of the Holy Spirit in reward for right faith in Christ, even if on account of human frailty his soul were to die for some sin or other, yet he will not die forever, but he will be raised by the grace of our Lord Jesus Christ Who *takes away the sin of the world* (John 1:29) and freely gives grace upon grace. Of this grace, which was manifested to the whole world and to our human race by the God-Man, it is said in the Gospel: *In Him was life, and the life was the light of men* (John 1:4), and further: *And the light shines in the darkness; and the darkness did not overpower it* (John 1:5). This means that the grace of the Holy Spirit which is granted at baptism in the name of the Father and the Son and the Holy Spirit, in spite of men's falls into sin, in spite of the darkness surrounding our soul, nevertheless shines in the heart with the divine light (which has existed from time immemorial) of the inestimable grace of Christ. In the event of a sinner's impenitence, this light of Christ cries to the Father: 'Abba, Father! Be not angry with this impenitence to the end (of his life).' And then, at the sinner's conversion to the way of repentance, it effaces completely all trace of past sin and clothes the former sinner once more in a robe of incorruption woven from the grace of the Holy Spirit, concerning the acquisition of which, as the aim of the Christian life, I have been speaking for so long to your Godliness.

"I will tell you something else, so that you may understand still more clearly what is meant by the grace of God, how to recognize it and how its action is manifested, particularly in those who are enlightened by it. The grace of the Holy Spirit is the light which enlightens man. The whole of Sacred Scripture speaks about this. Thus the Ancestor of God, David said: *Thy word is a lamp to my feet, and a light to my path* (Ps. 118:105), and *Unless Thy law had been my meditation I should have perished in my humiliation* (Ps. 118:92). In other words, the grace of the Holy Spirit which is expressed in the Law by the words of the Lord's commandments is my lamp and light. And if this grace of the Holy Spirit (which I try to acquire so carefully and zealously that I meditate on Thy righteous judgments seven times a day) did not enlighten me amidst the darkness of the cares which are inseparable from the high calling of my royal rank, whence should I get a spark of light to illumine my way on the path of life which is darkened by the ill will of my enemies?

"And in fact the Lord has frequently demonstrated before many witnesses how the grace of the Holy Spirit acts on people whom He has sanctified and illumined by His great inspirations.* Remember Moses after his talk with God on Mount Sinai. He so shone with an extraordinary light that people were unable to look at him. He was even forced to wear a veil when he appeared in public. Remember the Transfiguration of the Lord on Mount Tabor. A great light encircled Him, and *His raiment became shining, exceedingly white like snow* (Mark 9:3), and His disciples fell on their faces from fear. But when Moses and Elias appeared to Him in that light, a cloud overshadowed them in order to hide the radiance of the light of the divine grace which blinded the eyes of the disciples. Thus the grace of the All-Holy Spirit of God appears in an ineffable light to all to whom God reveals its action."

7.

THE PEACE AND WARMTH OF GRACE

B UT HOW," I asked Batiushka Seraphim, "can I know that I am in the grace of the Holy Spirit?"

"It is very simple, your Godliness," he replied. "That is why the Lord says: 'All things are simple to those who find knowledge.'** The trouble is that we do not seek this divine knowledge which does not puff up, for it is not of this world. This knowledge which is full of love for God and for our neighbor builds up every man for his salvation. Of this knowledge the Lord said

---

* Lit. "descents." Slavonic *naitie=epifitisis* (Greek).
** Proverbs 8:9 (Septuagint).

that God *wills all men to be saved, and to come to the knowledge of the truth* (I Tim. 2:4). And of the lack of this knowledge He said to His Apostles: *Are you also without understanding* (Matt. 15:16), or *have ye not read the Scriptures* (Matt. 21:42), or *did ye not understand this parable?* (Mark 4:13). Concerning this understanding, it is said in the Gospel of the Apostles: *Then opened He their understanding* (Luke 24:45), and the Apostles also perceived whether the Spirit of God was dwelling in them or not; and being filled with understanding, they saw the presence of the Holy Spirit with them and declared positively that their work was holy and entirely pleasing to the Lord God. That explains why in their epistles they wrote: *It seemed good to the Holy Spirit and to us* (Acts 15:28). Only on these grounds did they offer their epistles as immutable truth for the benefit of all the faithful. Thus the holy Apostles were consciously aware of the presence in themselves of the Spirit of God. And so you see, your Godliness, how simple it is!"

"Nevertheless," I replied, "I do not understand how I can be certain that I am in the Spirit of God. How can I discern for myself His true manifestation in me?"

Fr. Seraphim replied: "I have already told you, your Godliness, that it is very simple, and I have related in detail how people come to be in the Spirit of God and how we can recognize His presence in us. So what do you want, my dear?"

"I want to understand it well," I said.

Then Fr. Seraphim took me very firmly by the shoulders and said: "We are both in the Spirit of God now, my dear. Why don't you look at me?"

I replied: "I cannot look, Batiushka, because lightning is flashing from your eyes. Your face has become brighter than the sun, and my eyes ache with pain."

Fr. Seraphim said: "Don't be alarmed, your Godliness! Now you yourself have become as bright as I am. You are now in the fullness of the Spirit of God yourself; otherwise you would not be able to see me as I am."

Then bending his head towards me, he whispered softly in my ear: "Thank the Lord God for His unutterable mercy to you! You saw that I did not even cross myself; and only in my heart I prayed mentally to the Lord God and said within myself: 'Lord, grant him to see clearly with his bodily eyes that descent of Thy Spirit which Thou grantest to Thy servants when Thou art pleased to appear in the light of Thy magnificent glory.' And you see, my dear, the Lord instantly fulfilled the humble prayer of poor Seraphim. How then shall we not thank Him for this unspeakable gift to us both? Even to the greatest hermits, my dear, the Lord God does not always show His mercy in this way. This grace of God, like a loving mother, has been pleased to comfort your contrite heart at the intercession of the Mother of God herself. But why, my dear, do you not look me in the eyes? Just look, and don't be afraid! The Lord is with us!"

After these words I glanced at his face and there came over me an even greater reverent awe. Imagine in the center of the sun, in the dazzling light of its midday rays, the face of a man talking to you. You see the movement of his lips and the changing expression of his eyes, you hear his voice, you feel someone holding your shoulders; yet you do not see his hands, you do not even see yourself or his figure, but only a blinding light spreading far around for several yards and illumining with its glaring sheen both the snow blanket which covered the forest glade and the snowflakes which besprinkled me and the great Elder. You can imagine the state I was in!

"How do you feel now?" Fr. Seraphim asked me.

"Extraordinarily well," I said.

"But in what way? How exactly do you feel well?"

I answered: "I feel such calmness and peace in my soul that no words can express it."

"This, your Godliness," said Fr. Seraphim, "is that peace of which the Lord said to His disciples: *My peace I give to you; not as the world gives do I give to you* (John 14:27). *If you were of the world, the world would love its own; but because I have chosen you out of the world, therefore the world hates you* (John 15:19). *But be of good cheer; I have overcome the world* (John 16:33). And to those people whom this world hates but who are chosen by the Lord, the Lord gives that peace which you now feel within you, the peace which, in the words of the Apostles, *passes all understanding* (Phil. 4:7). The Apostle describes it in this way because it is impossible to express in words the spiritual well-being which it produces in those into whose hearts the Lord God has infused it. Christ the Savior calls it a peace which comes from His own generos-

St. Seraphim speaking to N. A. Motovilov.
Illustration from a book on the Saint by A. P. Timofievich.

ity and is not of this world, for no temporary earthly prosperity can give it to the human heart; it is granted from on high by the Lord God Himself, and that is why it is called the peace of God. What else do you feel?" Fr. Seraphim asked me.

"An extraordinary sweetness," I replied.

And he continued: "This is that sweetness of which it is said in Holy Scripture: *They will be inebriated with the fatness of Thy house; and Thou shalt make them drink of the torrent of Thy delight** (Ps. 35:8). And now this sweetness is flooding our hearts and coursing through our veins with unutterable delight. From this sweetness our hearts melt, as it were, and both of us are filled with such happiness as tongue cannot tell. What else do you feel?"

"An extraordinary joy in all my heart."

And Fr. Seraphim continued: "When the Spirit of God comes down to man and overshadows him with the fullness of His inspiration, then the human soul overflows with unspeakable joy, for the Spirit of God fills with joy whatever He touches. This is that joy of which the Lord speaks in His Gospel: *A woman when she is in travail has sorrow, because her hour is come; but when she is delivered of the child, she remembers no more the anguish, for joy that a man is born into the world. In the world you will be sorrowful,*** but when I see you again, your heart shall rejoice, and your joy no one will take from you* (John 16:21–22). Yet however comforting may be this joy which you now feel in your heart, it is nothing in comparison with that joy of which the Lord Himself by the mouth of His Apostle spoke: *Eye has not seen, nor ear heard, nor has it entered into the heart of man what God has prepared for them that love Him* (I Cor. 2:9). Foretastes of that joy are given to us now, and if they fill our souls with such sweetness, well-being and happiness, what shall we say of that joy which has been prepared in heaven for those who weep here on earth? And you, my dear, have wept enough in your life on earth; yet see with what joy the Lord consoles you even in this life! Now it is up to us, my dear, to add labors to labors in order to *go from strength to strength* (Ps. 83:7), and to come *to the measure of the stature of the fullness of Christ* (Eph. 4:13), so that the words

---

* The same word which in Slavonic means *delight* in Russian means *sweetness*.

** *In the world you will be sorrowful.* This is the Slavonic for *In the world you will have tribulation* (John 16:33). St. Seraphim has transposed it to its present context.

of the Lord may be fulfilled in us: *But they that wait upon the Lord shall renew their strength; they shall grow wings like eagles; and they shall run and not be weary; they shall walk and not faint* (Is. 40:31); *they will go from strength to strength, and the God of gods will appear to them in Sion* (Ps. 83:7) of understanding and heavenly visions. Only then will our present joy (which now visits us little and briefly) appear in all its fullness; and no one will take it from us, for we shall be filled to overflowing with inexplicable heavenly delights. What else do you feel, your Godliness?"

I answered: "An extraordinary warmth."

"How can you feel warmth, my dear? Look, we are sitting in the forest. It is winter out-of-doors, and snow is underfoot. There is more than an inch of snow on us, and the snowflakes are still falling. What warmth can there be?"

I answered: "Such as there is in a bathhouse when the water is poured on the stone and the steam rises in clouds."

"And the smell," he asked me, "is it the same as in a bathhouse?"

"No," I replied. "There is nothing on earth like this fragrance. When, in my dear mother's lifetime, I was fond of dancing and used to go to balls and parties, my mother would sprinkle me with scent that she bought at the best fashion shops in Kazan. But those scents did not exhale such fragrance."

And Fr. Seraphim, smiling pleasantly, said: "I know it myself just as well as you do, my dear, but I am asking you on purpose to see whether you feel it in the same way. It is absolutely true, your Godliness! The sweetest earthly fragrance cannot be compared with the fragrance which we now feel, for we are now enveloped in the fragrance of the Holy Spirit of God. What on earth can be like it? Mark, your Godliness, you have told me that around us it is warm as in the bathhouse. But look, neither on you nor me does the snow melt, nor does it underfoot; therefore, this warmth is not in the air but in us. It is that very warmth about which the Holy Spirit in the words of prayer makes us cry to the Lord: 'Warm me with the warmth of Thy Holy Spirit!' By it the hermits of both sexes were kept warm and did not fear the winter frost, being clad, as in fur coats, in the grace-given clothing woven by the Holy Spirit. And so it must be in actual fact, for the grace of God must dwell within us, in our heart, because the Lord said: *The Kingdom of God is within you* (Luke 17:21). By the Kingdom of God the Lord meant the grace of the Holy Spirit. This Kingdom of God is now within us, and the grace of the Holy Spirit shines upon and warms us from without as well. It fills the surrounding air with many fragrant odors, sweetens our senses with heavenly delight and floods our hearts with unutterable joy. Our present state is that of which the Apostle says: *The Kingdom of God is not food or drink, but righteousness and peace and joy in the Holy Spirit* (Rom. 14:17). Our faith consists not in the plausible words of earthly wisdom, but in the demonstration of the Spirit and power (cf. I Cor. 2:4). That is just the state we are in now. Of this state the Lord said: *There are some of those standing here who shall not taste of death till they see the Kingdom come in power* (Mark 9:11). See, your Godliness, what unspeakable joy the Lord God has now granted us! This is what it means to be in the fullness of the Holy Spirit. About this St. Macarius of Egypt writes: 'I myself was in the fullness of the Holy Spirit.' With this fullness of His Holy Spirit the Lord has now filled us poor creatures to overflowing. So there is no need now, your Godliness, to ask how people come to be in the grace of the Holy Spirit.... Will you be able to remember the present manifestation of God's ineffable mercy which has visited us?"

"I don't know, Father," I said, "whether the Lord will grant me to remember this mercy of God always as vividly and clearly as I feel it now."

"I think," Fr. Seraphim answered me, "that the Lord will help you to retain it in your memory forever, or His goodness would never have instantly bowed in this way to my humble prayer and so quickly anticipated the request of poor Seraphim; all the more so, because it is not given to you alone to understand it, but through you it is for the whole world, in order that you yourself may be confirmed in God's work and may be useful to others. The fact that I am a monk and you are a layman is utterly beside the point. What God requires is true faith in Himself and His only-begotten Son. In return for that the grace of the Holy Spirit is granted abundantly from on high. The Lord seeks a heart filled to overflowing with love for God and our neighbor; this is the throne on which He loves to sit and on which He appears in the fullness of His heavenly glory. 'Son, give me thy heart,' He says, 'and all the rest I Myself will add to thee'(cf. Prov. 23:26; Matt. 6:33), for in the human heart the Kingdom of God can be contained. The Lord commanded His disciples: *Seek first the Kingdom of God and His righteousness, and all these things shall be added to you; for your heavenly Father knows that you need all these things* (Matt. 6:33, 32). The Lord does not rebuke us for using earthly goods, for He says Himself that, owing to the conditions of our earthly life, we need all these things, that is, all the things which make our human life more peaceful and make our way to our heavenly home lighter and easier. That is why the holy Apostle Paul said that in his opinion there was nothing better on earth than piety and sufficiency (cf. II Cor. 9:8; I Tim. 6:6). And the Holy Church prays that this may be granted us by the Lord God; and though troubles, misfortunes and various needs are inseparable from our life on earth, yet the Lord God neither willed nor wills that we should have nothing but troubles and adversities. Therefore, He commands us through the Apostles to *bear one another's burdens and so fulfill the law of Christ* (Gal. 6:2). The Lord Jesus personally gives us the commandment to love one another so that by consoling one another with this mutual love, we may lighten the sorrowful and narrow way of our journey to the heavenly homeland. Why did He descend to us from heaven, if not for the purpose of taking upon Himself our poverty and of making us rich with the riches of His goodness and His unutterable generosity? He did not come to be served by men but to serve them Himself and to give life for the salvation of many. You do the same, your Godliness, and having seen the mercy of God manifestly shown to you, tell of it to all who desire salvation. *The harvest truly is great,* says the Lord, *but the laborers are few* (Luke 10:2). The Lord God has led us out to work and has given us the gifts of His grace in order that, by reaping the ears of the salvation of our fellowman and bringing as many as possible into the Kingdom of God, we may bring Him fruit—some thirty-fold, and some sixty-fold, and some a hundred-fold. Let us be watchful, my dear, in order that we may not be condemned with that wicked and slothful servant who hid his talent in the earth; but let us try to imitate those good and faithful servants of the Lord who brought their Master four talents instead of two, and ten instead of five (Matt. 25:14–30).

"Of the mercy of the Lord there is no shadow of doubt. You have seen for yourself, your Godliness, how the words of the Lord spoken through the Prophet have been accomplished in us: 'I am not a God far off, but a God near at hand' (cf. Jer. 23:23), and 'thy salvation is at thy mouth' (cf. Deut. 30:12–14; Rom. 10:8–13). I had not time even to cross myself, but only wished in my heart that the Lord would grant you to see His goodness in all its fullness, and He was pleased to hasten to realize my wish. I am not boasting when I say this, neither do I say it to show you my importance and lead you to jealousy, or to make you think that I am a monk and you only a layman. No, no, your Godliness: *The Lord is near to all who call upon Him in truth* (Ps. 144:18), *and there is no partiality with Him* (Eph. 6:9). For the Father loves the Son and gives everything into His hand (cf. John 3:35). If only we ourselves loved Him, our Heavenly Father, in a truly filial way! The Lord listens equally to the monk and the simple Christian layman provided that both are Orthodox, and both love God from the depths of their souls and have faith in Him, if only as a grain of mustard seed; and they both shall move mountains. 'One shall move thousands and two tens of thousands' (cf. Deut. 32:30). The Lord Himself says: *All things are possible to him who believes* (Mark 9:23). And the holy Apostle Paul loudly exclaims: *I can do all things in Christ who strengthens me* (Phil. 4:13). But does not our Lord Jesus Christ speak even more wonderfully than this of those who believe in Him: *He who believes in Me,* not only *the works that I do,* but even *greater than these shall he do, because I am going to My Father. And I will pray* for you *that your joy may be full. Hitherto you have asked nothing in My name.* But now *ask and ye shall receive…* (John 14:12, 16; 16:24).

"Thus, your Godliness, whatever you ask of the Lord God, you will receive, if only it is for the glory of God or for the good of your neighbor, because what we do for the good of our neighbor He refers to His own glory. And therefore He says: 'All that you have done to one of the least of these you have done to Me' (cf. Matt. 25:40). And so, have no doubt that the Lord God will fulfill your petitions, if only they concern the glory of God or the benefit and edification of your fellowman. But even if something is necessary for your own need or use or advantage, just as quickly and graciously will the Lord God be pleased to send you even that, provided that extreme need and necessity require it. For the Lord loves those who love Him. The Lord is good to all men; He gives abundantly to those who call upon His name, and His bounty is in all His works. He will do the will of them that fear Him, and He will hear their prayer and fulfill all their plans. The Lord will fulfill all thy petitions (cf. Ps. 144:19, 19:4–5). Only beware, your Godliness, of asking the Lord for something for which there is no urgent need. The Lord will not refuse you even this return for your Orthodox faith in Christ the Saviour, for the Lord will not give up the staff of the righteous to the lot of sinners (cf. Ps. 124:3), and He will speedily accomplish the will of His servant David; but He will call him to account for having troubled Him without special need and having asked Him for something without which he could have managed very easily.

"And so, your Godliness, I have now told you and given you a practical demonstration of all that the Lord and the Mother of God have been pleased to tell and show you through me, poor Seraphim. Now go in peace. The Lord and the Mother of God be with you always, now and ever, and to the ages of ages. Amen. Now go in peace."

And during the whole of this time, from the moment when Fr. Seraphim's face became radiant,* this illumination continued; and all that he told me from the beginning of the narrative until now, he said while remaining in one and the same position. The ineffable glow of the light which emanated from him I myself saw with my own eyes. And I am ready to vouch for it with an oath.

NOTE**

A T THIS POINT the Motovilov manuscript comes to an end. The depth of meaning of this document of the triumph of Orthodoxy can neither be explained nor underscored by means of my pen. It needs no testimony for itself because it testifies on its own behalf with such unconquerable might. Its significance cannot be diminished by the superfluous words of this world.

---

* Or, "became illuminated," "began to shine."
** The Note and Afterword have been taken from *Russian Pilgrim*, vol. 33, no. 2, 1990, pp. 90–92, in Russian.

But if only one could have seen in what condition the papers of Motovilov came down to me, which preserved in their ciphers this precious testimony of the God-pleasing life of the holy Elder! The dust stains, pigeon feathers and bird droppings, scraps of totally uninteresting bills, copies of agricultural leases with vouchers, letters of other people—all in a single heap, stacked crisscross and weighing about 100 pounds. All the papers were old, totally covered with scribbling and such a degree of illegible handwriting that I was simply overwhelmed: how was I ever to make sense of it?

In analyzing this chaos, encountering every possible obstacle, especially his scrawl which was for me a stumbling stone, I remember nearly falling into despondency. Here amidst all this gibberish, time and again, like a spark shooting out in the darkness, I caught sight, with difficulty, of the cryptic phrase: "Batiushka Seraphim said to me ..." What did he say? What did these unsolved hieroglyphics conceal within themselves? I became despondent.

I recall before evening, after an entire day of persistent and fruitless labor, that I ran out of patience and begged: "Fr. Seraphim, why have you given me the opportunity to receive the manuscript of your 'servant' in so distant a place as Diveyevo if, undecipherable, it will return again to oblivion?" My cry must have come from my soul. In the morning, taking up the papers for examination, I immediately found this manuscript and received the ability to make out Motovilov's handwriting. It is not hard to imagine my joy and how significant these words of the manuscript were to me: "'And I think,' Fr. Seraphim answered me, 'that the Lord will enable you forever to retain this in your memory, for otherwise His grace would never have inclined so instantly in this way to my humble prayer and so quickly anticipated the request of poor Seraphim; all the more so, because it is not given to you alone to understand it, but through you to the whole world....'"

For seventy long years has this treasure lain under a bushel in the attic, amidst various forgotten rubbish. How long was it to be before it came into print? Until right before the very glorification of the holy relics of him whom the Orthodox Church now begins to entreat: "Holy Father Seraphim, pray to God for us."

S. A. Nilus
May 19, 1903

AFTERWORD

THE FIRST APPEARANCE in print of the manuscript of N. A. Motovilov, entitled by me "The Holy Spirit Clearly Resting on Fr. Seraphim of Sarov in his Conversation on the Aim of the Christian Life with the Simbirsk Landowner and Judicial Counselor, Nicholas Alexandrovich Motovilov," evoked, to my great sorrow and, at the same time, to the exposure of the "spirit of the times," many bewildering commentaries. These appeared even in that milieu which by the grace of preaching must, it would seem, stand at the head of the fiery coal of the Orthodox Church. The human heart, overcome by vanity, according to all indications, cannot find a place within itself for that revelation, in all its fullness, which is contained in the priceless words of the manuscript testimony of the sharer of mysteries with St. Seraphim, and refuses to receive and believe the possibility of the manifestation of the activity of the descent of the Holy Spirit of God in all its fullness witnessed in a mortal man.

"You, together with Motovilov, are preaching after the manner of the sectarian Labzin who sprang up during that well-known period of the reign of Alexander I, when people wanted to see the grace of the Holy Spirit only in its visible manifestation: in warmth, in light and in fragrance. From here it is not too far to 'delusion'!" Such statements I managed to hear soon after the appearance of Motovilov's manuscript in print.

I ask for forgiveness from all Orthodox Christians who might have been plunged into tempting perplexity by the small labor of the writer, but the guilt is mine only in so far as I did not emphasize with sufficient force that the sensible manifestation of the grace of the Holy Spirit which settled upon St. Seraphim was given to the enlightened vision of Motovilov only at the prayers of the Elder, and at the prayers of the same holy Elder the vision as well as the divinely-inspired conversation was preserved in the memory of Motovilov "not only for him, but through him for the whole world." There is not and there cannot be anything similar between self-proclaimed sectarian Labzin and Motovilov, who throughout his entire life remained in communication with and under the guidance of elders, one of whom has been glorified by the Holy Church as a God-pleaser and saint, and the other (Archbishop

Anthony of Voronezh) is similarly revered by all Orthodox-believing hearts. The initial and, one may say, fundamental sign of sectarianism and "delusion" is whim; and this is precisely what is lacking in the given case.

But let us turn rather in this regard to the testimony of the Church herself in the person of her trustworthy saints. This is how St. Theognostus bears witness: "Even though through constantly abiding in pure prayer, which immaterially unites the immaterial intellect together with God, you are vouchsafed to see, as in a mirror, the blessed state which awaits you at the completion of the present life, you are vouchsafed this, as having received the betrothal of the Spirit and as having acquired the heavenly kingdom within yourself, in the clearest manner and by the most distinct cleansing of your soul; but do not suffer to be separated from the flesh without foreknowledge of your approaching death. Pray unceasingly about this and be in good hope that you will receive this news when your end draws nigh, if this is for your profit" (Chapter 75).*

By the content of these words of St. Theognostus, the Hierarch Ignatius Brianchaninov in his "Homily on Death," reasons thus:

"Spiritual perception, about which St. Theognostus speaks, is quite fairly termed in the patristic writings 'revelation' because of its quality of decisive verification. It initiates illumination by divine grace that received into the Fatherly spiritual embrace both the repentant and the bewildered sinner. It appears in the soul unexpectedly, like new life about which a man until then could not have obtained the slightest understanding. It frees the soul from the onslaught of evil spirits and passions; it transforms the entire man in that wondrous moment in which God's Spirit calls out to God from the man. All the bones of that man shall say with ineffable spiritual thanksgiving and doxology: *Lord, O Lord, who is like unto Thee? Thou hast delivered the beggar from the hands of them that are stronger than he, yea, the poor man and the pauper from them that despoil him* (Ps. 34:11–12). *The soul of such a man shall rejoice in the Lord, it shall delight in His salvation* (Ps. 34:10). Spiritual perception is so powerful that, filling a man, it removes from him sympathy for all other

---

* "Ascetical Works of St. Theognostus," *Christian Reading,* 1826, p. 23, in Russian. Also, St. Theognostus, "On the Practice of the Virtues," *The Philokalia,* vol. 2 (London: Faber and Faber, 1981), p. 377.

matters; or to put it more concisely, it is the indwelling in the soul of the Kingdom of God. Having acquired this perception *he shall not henceforth live unto himself* (II Cor. 5:15) but to God. The opinion of such perception among those subject to self-delusion and demonic prelest is to be distinguished from grace-filled perception by the contrary fruits."[*]

And thus let us be no longer troubled in heart; and may we through the guidance and by the prayers of our elders, our spiritual fathers, acquire the grace of the Holy Spirit in those ways, known to Him alone, in which He will be well-pleased to condescend to us sinners. It is necessary to remember that the manner of the illumination of the Holy Spirit, which the talk of Fr. Seraphim treated and which was set forth by his great disciple N. A. Motovilov, was, according to the expression of the saint himself, "not always given even to the great hermits by the Lord's mercy." Oh, what a triumph of our faith! But what else yet awaits her, when the times and seasons will be fulfilled!…

Yea, come Lord Jesus!

S. A. Nilus
1911

---

[*] Bishop Ignatius Brianchaninov, "Homily on Death," *Collected Works,* vol. 3, 3rd ed. (St. Petersburg, 1905), pp. 147–48, in Russian.

St. Seraphim blessing a pilgrim while on his way from his hermitage
to the monastery. Lithograph by the Fesenko studio, 1903.

III

The Great Diveyevo Mystery

Procession during the glorification of St. Seraphim, with Tsar Nicholas II and other members of the royal family bearing the relics of the Saint. Lithograph from Diveyevo Convent, 1903.

PREFACE

W HEN ON THE EVE of St. Seraphim's canonization the manuscripts of Motovilov, that friend of St. Seraphim, so close to him in spirit, became comprehensible to Sergei Nilus, he stood in awe. Before him hitherto unknown mysteries were revealed in a wondrous manner, preserving the words of one of the great saints of Christendom. He understood their universal significance and, having transcribed them, he sent them to the ecclesiastical press, to Bishop Nikon of Vologda, so that before the very glorification Orthodox Russia might be forewarned of that which awaited her.

Out of all that had been found in the notes of Motovilov, the only thing that was allowed by the censor to be printed was what is now known as the "Conversation of St. Seraphim on the Aim of the Christian Life"; all the remaining material had apparently disappeared (especially after the Communist destruction) without a trace, with the exception of those priceless grains, the words of St. Seraphim which Nilus managed to include in his wonderful writings.

In a such a way, aside from the biography of Motovilov himself (compiled by Sergei Nilus and placed in his book *Greatness in Small Things*) and the aforementioned "Conversation," there were published in his books which came out in 1917 only a couple of pages from the notes, under the heading: "Concerning the Fate of True Christians."

And thus things would have remained, if it had not been for his niece, Helen Yurievna Kontzevitch, who preserved certain of his manuscripts, unpublished chapters of his book *On the Bank of God's River*. One of these chapters was entitled "The Mystery of Diveyevo."

Not long before his death, not wishing to leave his native land, Sergei Alexandrovich Nilus sent the manuscripts abroad to his niece so that she might publish them. He even exacted a promise from her, saying that if she did not do it, she would be held liable for this in the next world. The aforementioned chapter, however, contained extraordinary information which the pre-revolutionary censor considered to be risky to publish in an age of skepticism, so as not to harm the work of the glorification of the God-pleaser of Sarov. However, once the Russian Empire had collapsed, it became impossible to print anything spiritual at all in Russia. Abroad, Helen Yurievna was advised even more strongly not to print the manuscript, so as not to undermine the faith of the remnant of downtrodden émigré believers. She awaited a more favorable time, which did not appear—and time went by. A half-century after the day of the glorification of St. Seraphim, she attempted to publish the Mystery, but was unable. Her uncle even appeared to her in a dream and threatened her, but she still had no opportunity to do so.

Months prior to the founding of the St. Herman Brotherhood, the future brothers visited Ivan Mikhailovich Kontzevitch, Helen's husband, who was dying. It was the day of the commemoration of St. Herman, who was then not as yet canonized a saint. Almost on his deathbed, Ivan Mikhailovich implored them to help his future widow in one very important matter of universal significance. Helen Yurievna explained the situation of the manuscript to them. Understanding that the time was propitious to do so, they promised to publish Nilus' book. With the blessing of the righteous Archbishop Averky (Taushev) of Holy Trinity Monastery in Jordanville, New York, who had himself wanted to publish the book, they printed the second volume of *On the Bank of God's River*, where this Mystery was placed in the eighth chapter. This first publication in the Russian language in book form by the St. Herman Brotherhood soon reached Russia. It has since become known throughout Russia, where it has been reprinted in many different publications.

It is not for us to judge the meaning of this Mystery. The mysteries of God are revealed to individuals according to the degree of their spiritual maturity. The resurgence of Orthodoxy that has taken place in Russia since the fall of Communism is undoubtedly of great spiritual significance for the entire world. Thus, that worldwide evil which is ever increasing and threatens to inundate the remaining number of the righteous, may perhaps be dispersed in an instant, like a thundercloud, by the breath from the lips of God, if those who believe in Him have repentance and hope in His mercy towards His chosen people, the new Israel, the people of the Christian race.

We offer, therefore, this translation from the book published earlier by us, of the testimonial words, which speak much to today's Orthodox, of our dear St. Seraphim of Sarov, the meek slave of the Living God.

St. Herman of Alaska Brotherhood

Concerning the Fate
of True Christians

Written down by Motovilov on the night of
October 26–27, 1844

ONCE I WAS IN GREAT SORROW, reflecting on what would happen to our Orthodox Church if the evil of our time would continue to increase more and more; and being convinced that our Church was in an extremely lamentable condition, both because of the immorality of the flesh which was increasing, and likewise—if not indeed even much more so—because of the impiety of spirit through the godless philosophies which were being spread everywhere by the newest false teachers, I very much desired to know what Batiushka Seraphim would tell me about this.

After having spoken in detail about the holy Prophet Elijah, he answered my question, among other things, in the following way:

"Elijah the Tishbite, in complaining to the Lord against Israel that in its entirety it had bent the knee to Baal, said in prayer that he alone, Elijah, had remained faithful to the Lord, but they were already seeking to take away his soul, also.... And what, Batiushka, did the Lord answer him?—*I have left seven thousand men in Israel who have not bent the knee to Baal* (I Kings 19:18). And so, if in the kingdom of Israel, which had fallen away from the kingdom of Judea which was faithful to God and had become completely corrupted, there remained still seven thousand men faithful to the Lord, then what shall we say of Russia? I suppose that in the kingdom of Israel at that time there were no more than three million people. And how many, Batiushka, are there now in our Russia?"

I replied: "About sixty million." And he continued:

"Twenty times more. Then judge for yourself how many we have now who are still faithful to God! So it is, Batiushka, so it is: Whom He did foreknow, He also did forechoose; and whom He did forechoose, He also did predestinate; and whom He did predestinate, He will also watch over and glorify. And so, what is there for us to be downcast about!... God is with us! (cf. Rom. 8:29–31). *He that trusteth in the Lord shall be as Mount Zion ... and the Lord is round about His people* (Ps. 124:1–2). *The Lord shall preserve thy going out and thy coming in from this time forth even forevermore; ... the sun shall not smite thee by day nor the moon by night* (Ps. 120:6–8).

And then I asked him what this means, and why he was saying this to me.

"Because," Batiushka Seraphim replied, "in this same way the Lord will preserve, as the apple of His eye, His people, that is, Orthodox Christians who love Him and serve Him with all their heart and all their mind, both in word and deed, day and night. And such are they who preserve entirely all the rules, dogmas, and traditions of our Eastern Orthodox Church, and who with their lips confess the piety which has been handed down by the Church, and who act in very deed in all circumstances of life according to the holy commandments of our Lord Jesus Christ."

In confirmation of the fact that there remain yet many in the Russian land who are faithful to our Lord Jesus Christ and who live piously in an Orthodox way, Batiushka Seraphim said once to an acquaintance of mine—either Fr. Gurias, who was the guest master of Sarov, or Fr. Symeon, who was in charge of the Masleshchensky Yard—that once, being in the Spirit, he saw the whole Russian land, and it was filled and, as it were, covered with the smoke of the prayers of the faithful who were praying to the Lord....

In one of his conversations with Motovilov, St. Seraphim, speaking about the spiritual state of the last Christians who will remain faithful to God before the end of the world, related something highly important for the support of the remnant of the confessors of Christ:

"And in the days of that great sorrow, of which it is said that no flesh would be saved unless, for the sake of the elect, those days will be cut short—in those days the remnant of the faithful are to experience in themselves something like that which was experienced once by the Lord Himself when He, hanging on the Cross, being perfect God and perfect Man, felt Himself so forsaken by His Divinity that He cried out to Him: *My God, My God, why hast Thou forsaken Me* (Matt. 24:46). The last Christians also will experience in themselves a similar abandonment of humanity by the grace of God, but only for a very short time, after the passing of which the Lord will not delay to appear immediately in all His glory, and all the holy angels with Him. And then will be performed in all its fulness everything foreordained from the ages in the pre-eternal counsel [of the Holy Trinity]."

The Great Diveyevo Mystery

From the Eighth Chapter of *On the Bank of God's River*
by S. A. Nilus

I WILL NOW MAKE KNOWN what I have preserved up to now in my heartfelt memory, for, I think, God's appointed time had not yet arrived. But if my inner presentiments do not deceive me, these times have now been fulfilled; and the time has come to reveal to the world of believers and unbelievers a noetic pearl, treasured until now and hidden by me, the likes of which the world has not known since the days of the Greek Emperor Theodosius the Younger. The resurrection of Lazarus is known to each Christian. About the resurrection of the seven youths very few know; and therefore, before the disclosure of the great mystery of St. Seraphim (which I call the Diveyevo Mystery—the place of its manifestation), I will in brief communicate to the uninformed the story of the seven youths.

These seven noble youths: Maximilian, Exacustodian, Jamblicus, Martinian, Dionysius, John and Antoninus, linked one to another equally by military service as by close friendship and faith, during the time of Decius' persecution of the Christians of Ephesus (around the year 250) hid in a mountain cave, called Ochlon, near the city of Ephesus in Asia Minor. In this cave they spent their time in fasting and prayer, preparing for the feat of martyrdom for Christ. Having learned about the hiding place of the youths, Decius ordered that the entrance be walled up with stones in order to give the confessors over to death by starvation.

After the passage of more than 170 years, in the reign of Theodosius the Younger (408–450), a true defender of the faith, the entrance to the cave opened up and the blessed youths arose, yet not for martyrdom, but rather to

St. Seraphim's belongings, which are treasured in Diveyevo.
From *The Diveyevo Chronicles.*

put to shame unbelievers who denied the actual resurrection of the dead. Upon being informed of this great miracle, Emperor Theodosius arrived from Constantinople with his dignitaries and a multitude of people in Ephesus, where he found these youths still among the living and bowed before them, as before the most wondrous testimony of the future general Resurrection.

According to the testimony of the church historian Nicephorus Callistus, the Emperor was in contact with them for seven days, conversed with them and even served them at table. After the passage of these days the youths again slept the sleep of death until the Dread Judgment of the Lord and the general Resurrection. Their holy relics were glorified by many miracles.

This account independently from church tradition also carries weighty testimony because of its own historical reliability. St. John Kolovos, a contemporary of the event, speaks about it in the life of St. Paisius the Great (commemorated on June 19th). The Marionite Syrians, who separated themselves from the Orthodox Church in the seventh century, honor in their services the holy youths. They are found in the Ethiopian Calendar and in the ancient Roman Martyrologies. Their history was known to Mohammed and to many Arab writers. St. Gregory of Tours states that these men until his day reposed in that very spot, clothed in silk and long linen raiment. The cave of the youths until the present could be seen near Ephesus at the edge of Mt. Priona. The fate of their relics is unknown since the twelfth century, at the beginning of which Abbot Daniel saw them still in the cave.

Having been saved from death by a miracle of St. Seraphim in 1902, out of faith I traveled at the beginning of that same year to Sarov and Diveyevo to thank the saint for my salvation. And there, at Diveyevo, with the blessing of the great Diveyevo Eldress Abbess Maria and at the behest of Elena Ivanovna Motovilova, I received a large basket of all kinds of papers, which had been left after the death of Nicholas Alexandrovich Motovilov, containing various notes in his own hand. Amongst these notes I found this priceless treasure, this "noetic pearl," which I call the Mystery of Diveyevo—the Mystery of St. Seraphim, Wonderworker of Sarov and all Russia.

Here I transcribe the notes which I found:

"The great Elder Batiushka Seraphim," thus writes Motovilov, "speaking with me about his flesh (he never called his flesh 'relics'), mentioned the name of the Most Pious Sovereign Nicholas, his Most Devout Consort Alexandra Fyodorovna and his mother, the Dowager Empress Maria Fyodorovna. Recalling the Sovereign Nicholas, he said, 'He is in soul a Christian.'"

From the various notes, part in notebooks, part on scraps of paper, it was possible to suppose that not a little energy had been applied by Motovilov to the end that the glorification of the saint could be celebrated during the reign of Nicholas I, his consort Alexandra Fyodorovna and his mother Maria Fyodorovna. And great was his disappointment when his efforts were not crowned with success, contrary, as it seemed, to the prediction of the God-pleaser, which linked his glorification with the indicated combination of royal names.

Motovilov died in 1879, not having lived to see the justification of his faith. Could he or anyone else have guessed that within 48 years of the death of Nicholas I the very same names would appear on the throne of all Russia: Nicholas, Alexandra Fyodorovna and Maria Fyodorovna, during whose reign the foretold glorification, which Motovilov so cherished, of the great seer St. Seraphim would take place?

In another place in the notes of Motovilov, I found the following Great Mystery of Diveyevo:

Many times I heard from the mouth of the great God-pleaser, the Elder, Fr. Seraphim, that he would not lie in Sarov with his flesh. And behold, once I (Motovilov) dared to ask him: "Batiushka, you deign to say all the time that with your flesh you will not lie in Sarov. Does that mean that the monks of Sarov will give you away?"

To this Batiushka, smiling pleasantly and looking at me, deigned to reply to me thus: "O your Godliness, your Godliness, what are you saying! For, why was Tsar Peter a king of kings and wanted to translate the relics of the holy pious Prince Alexander Nevsky to Petersburg, but the holy relics did not want this?"

"How did they not want it?" I dared to answer the great Elder. "How did they not want it, when they repose now in Petersburg in the Lavra of St. Alexander Nevsky?"

"In the St. Alexander Nevsky Lavra, you say? But how can that be? In Vladimir they reposed openly, but in the Lavra they are buried—why is that? Because," said Batiushka, "they are not there." And after speaking much in detail on this subject with his divinely-speaking lips, Batiushka Seraphim informed me of the following:

"Your Godliness, the Lord God has ordained that I, humble Seraphim, should live considerably longer than a hundred years. But since by that time the bishops will become so impious that in their impiety they will surpass the Greek bishops of the time of Theodosius the Younger, so that they will no longer even believe in the chief dogma of the Christian faith, therefore it has been pleasing to the Lord God to take me, humble Seraphim, from this temporal life until the time, and then resurrect me; and my resurrection will be as the resurrection of the Seven Youths in the cave of Ochlon in the days of Theodosius the Younger."

Having revealed to me this great and fearful mystery, the great Elder informed me that after his resurrection he would go from Sarov to Diveyevo, and there he would begin preaching worldwide repentance. For this preaching, and above all because of the miracle of resurrection, a great multitude of people will assemble from all the ends of the earth; Diveyevo will become a Lavra, Vertyanova will become a city, and Arzamas a province. And preaching repentance in Diveyevo, Batiushka Seraphim will uncover four relics in it; and after uncovering them, he himself will lie down in their midst. And then soon will come the end of everything.

This great Diveyevo mystery of piety was discovered by me in the handwritten notes of the Simbirsk judicial Counselor, Nicholas Alexandrovich Motovilov, the sharer of mysteries with the great seer of prophetic stature, our venerable and God-bearing Father Seraphim, Wonderworker of Sarov and all Russia.

In supplementing this mystery, here is what I heard from the lips of the 84-year-old Diveyevo Abbess Maria. I was with her at the beginning of August, 1903, right after the glorification of St. Seraphim and the departure from Diveyevo of the Royal Family. I congratulated her with the justification of her great faith (Matushka, having built the Diveyevo Catholicon, had omitted consecrating the left side altar since 1880, believing, in harmony with Diveyevo tradition, that she would live until Fr. Seraphim's glorification and could consecrate the side altar to his holy name); I congratulated her, but she said to me:

"Yes, my dear father, Sergei Alexandrovich, it is a great miracle. But there will be a greater miracle, and such a miracle. That is, just as the procession with the cross now went from Diveyevo to Sarov, so will it go from Sarov to Diveyevo: 'And there will be so many people,' as spake our God-pleaser, St. Seraphim, 'as there are ears in a field. That will be a miracle of miracles, a wonder of wonders.'"

"How is this to be understood, Matushka?" I asked, having at that time totally forgotten about the already-known to me great Diveyevo mystery concerning the resurrection of the venerable one.

"And thus, whoever lives until then, the same will see it," Abbess Maria replied to me, intently looking at me and smiling.

This was my last visit on earth with the great carrier of the Diveyevo tradition, Abbess Maria, "of the Ushakov family," the twelfth Superior; a little more than thirty years after his death, according to the prophecy of St. Seraphim, Diveyevo, this future women's Lavra, would become a Convent.

Within a year after this meeting Abbess Maria reposed in the Lord.*

---

* S. A. Nilus, *On the Bank of God's River,* vol. 2 (San Francisco: St. Herman of Alaska Brotherhood, 1969), pp. 192–93, in Russian.

Abbess Maria of Diveyevo.
From *The Diveyevo Chronicles.*

St. Seraphim's Prophecy on the Resurrection of Russia

COUNTESS NATALIA VLADIMIROVNA URUSOVA, personally known to the founders of the St. Herman Brotherhood, was in correspondence with Helen Y. Kontzevitch, who left them the letters as well as the memoirs of the late Countess. This is what she communicates therein:

"I knew of the prophecy of St. Seraphim about the fall and resurrection of Russia; I knew it personally. When at the beginning of 1918 Yaroslavl burned, I fled with my children to Sergiev Posad and there became acquainted with Count [Y. A.] Olsufyev,* then comparatively young. In order to save documents which would have been destroyed by the diabolical power of Bolshevism, he managed to situate them in the library of the Holy Trinity—St. Sergius Academy. Soon he was shot. He once brought me a letter to read through, with the words: 'I have preserved this as the apple of my eye.' The letter, yellow with age, with severely faded ink, had been written by the very hand of the holy St. Seraphim of Sarov to Motovilov.

"In the letter was a prophecy concerning those horrors and misfortunes which would befall Russia, and I only remember what was said in it about both the pardon and salvation of Russia. I do not remember the year, since 28 years have passed by; my memory might betray me. I repent that I did not read it with the necessary attention since the year was indicated remotely; but we longed for salvation and deliverance immediately after the very onset of the revolution, and it seems that is was 1947—in any case, in the last years of

---

* A founding member, together with Priest Paul Florensky, of the "Commission for the Preservation of Monuments of Culture and Antiquity of the Holy Trinity-St. Sergius Lavra."

the 20th century. I cannot forgive myself that I did not make a copy from that letter; but my head was so crowded and my brains so worn out in quests for the daily needs of my children, that only by this am I able to be at ease and justify my nearsightedness…. I remember the letter well."

Early 20th-century icon of St. Seraphim. Lithograph on metal.

APPENDIX I

St. Seraphim in Bonds

THE DESTRUCTION OF
THE GREAT SAROV MONASTERY

*Remember that Jesus Christ of the seed of David
is risen again from the dead, according to my gospel,
wherein I suffer trouble, as an evil-doer, even unto
bonds; but the word of God is not bound.*
II Tim. 2:8–9

HAVING SURVIVED the first years of the Revolution and the terrible trials of persecution and the apostasy of the "Living Church," St. Seraphim's Sarov Monastery and Diveyevo Convent were closed by the Communists in 1927. Only partial information has come down to us concerning the suffering and fate of the many holy monks and nuns who lived in these monasteries at that time, but what has come down is enough to form a separate chapter in the history of Russia's new martyrs. Here is what is known of some of the leading Sarov monks:

ABBOT HIEROTHEUS was the abbot of Sarov during the canonization of St. Seraphim in 1903; then he retired and led an ascetic life until he was sent by the Communists to Temnikov prison (the former Sanaxar Monastery), where he met his suffering and death.

ABBOT RUFINUS. In 1927, after the closure of the Monastery, he was arrested and imprisoned in the prison of Arzamas, where he was cruelly tortured. According to the testimony of those who were with him in prison, once when he was brought back to his cell after a long interrogation, none of the prisoners could recognize him. His whole face was swollen, especially under the chin. All of the hair of his beard had been pulled out. Soon after this he was tortured to death.*

MONK BASIL, a severe ascetic. His obedience was to stay always by the spring of St. Seraphim and dispense holy water to the pilgrims. During the destruction of the Monastery, the atheist "activists" made a bonfire in the middle of the Monastery, threw into it icons and other holy objects after sacrilegiously trampling on them, and burned the log coffin which had been made by the saint himself and in which his relics had reposed for seventy years until his canonization. Then they destroyed both of the log cabins in the saint's "Near" and "Far" Hermitages, and having defiled his spring and muddied it, they martyred Father Basil, who died as a true monk—at his obedience.**

MONK ISAAC. A clairvoyant Elder who was known to the whole of Orthodox Russia, it was through him that St. Seraphim revealed to the monks what to do with his holy relics. At the time of the destruction of the Monastery, "the monks resisted the taking away of the holy relics and locked themselves in the Dormition Church where the relics of the saint lay, declaring that they would all be killed rather than give up the relics. For three days the monks remained locked up in the church without eating.… In Sarov at that time lived the ascetic, Father Isaac, a disciple and successor of the renowned Elder Anatole (of Sarov), who died in 1922. Elder Isaac, grieving over what was happening and having pity on the brethren, prayed to the saint for three days that he would instruct them how to act. On the third day St. Seraphim appeared to him and said: 'It is the will of God that my relics be taken away from here and the Monastery destroyed; do not hinder this.' When the Elder told this vision to the brethren, the monks left the church, and the commission of secret police agents and local Soviet 'experts,' having gathered the relics into a wooden box, took them away; and the monks in the

---

* Archpriest Michael Polsky, *Russia's New Martyrs,* vol. 2 (Jordanville, New York: Holy Trinity Monastery, 1957), p. 228, in Russian.
** Ibid.

evening of February 9, 1927, were all driven away from Sarov, and in this way the Sarov Hermitage ended its existence.... The relics of St. Seraphim were taken to Moscow and placed in the Rumyantsev Museum (converted into an anti-religious museum); and in the newspapers it was announced that the bones of Seraphim of Sarov had been brought, and those who wished could view them. The people began to come in masses to the museum to venerate the holy relics. Tickets were sold for admission to the museum costing three rubles; but despite this high charge the people came, wept, prayed, and bowed down before the glass cover under which the relics lay. There were many healings. Then the Communists, seeing that not a mockery, but rather a glorification of the holy relics was occurring, announced that the relics were no longer in the museum, but had been taken away to the city of Penza. The faithful were not satisfied with this announcement, and many went to Penza to be convinced for themselves; but in Penza it was announced to them that there were no relics there. Thus the relics of St. Seraphim were hidden, and now it is not known where they are."*

In Russia it was widely believed that the relics of the saint were stolen from the train which was taking them away from Moscow and were hidden by members of the Catacomb Church.**

The fate of Sarov Monastery and the continued presence of St. Seraphim there after its closure are described in the memoirs of the Nun Veronica, who was a prisoner in the hospital of one of the concentration camps in St. Seraphim's forest near the Monastery: "Around our barracks, as a thick green wall, stood a forest of age-old pines. Amidst the columns of their red trunks was the bright emerald green of curving birches—the unforgettable Sarov forest, unique in the world. Involuntarily we all the felt the invisible power and the grace-filled nearness of the holy Monastery. The saint himself appeared once on a road in the forest to a sick monk-prisoner when he became exhausted under the weight of his burden and could not go on. Almost all the believing prisoners experienced St. Seraphim's help in their own lives. They felt his protection and defense in the midst of the most difficult trials.

---

* Hieromonk George of Sarov, from the words of Abbot Methodius, an eyewitness. *Messenger of the Russian Student Christian Movement,* May-June, 1934, p. 20, in Russian.

** See Appendix II below for a recounting of what actually happened to the saint's relics.

At first a concentration camp was built in the Monastery. But such a despondency attacked the officials of the 'special division' who were sent there, and so frequent did cases of suicide among them become, that the camp was transferred to another place; and in the Monastery an orphanage for the children of prisoners was established. It is related that at night the children often see an elder in a white garment and a black half-mantle."*

Diveyevo Convent was closed by the Communists in September, 1927, some months after Sarov. Here is how its end was described by Mother Alexandra, as recorded by Dr. A. P. Timofievich:** "For several months before the closure, there were signs in the Monastery. Sometimes the bells would ring by themselves; sometimes the main church would be all illuminated inside at night, and everyone would become alarmed and think there was a fire. But then everything would again be quiet and dark, and this happened many times. But when our Blessed one (Maria, the clairvoyant Fool-for-Christ) made a great uproar and began to prophesy clearly that a disaster was coming—then our eldest nuns assembled and decided to hide all of the saint's holy things, distributing them to trustworthy people. Everything was taken away.***

"'And what about the chief holy object,' I asked, 'the wonderworking Icon of the Mother of God of Tender Feeling (*Umileniye*)? Was it saved?'

"The Lord helped to save it too; and we believe that His wrath is not unto the end, and that when the Monastery will arise from the ashes, the Icon also will return to its place. Earlier an exact copy of the Icon was made and was placed in a metal covering; but the original has been taken far away, where the hand of the blasphemer will not reach it."

And so Sarov and Diveyevo Monasteries were destroyed, the vast forest of Sarov chopped down, the saint's relics mocked, and his very memory as it were abolished from the face of the Russian land. And yet, Sarov and Diveyevo Monasteries are specifically mentioned in the prophecies of St. Sera-

---

* *St. Vladimir's Russian National Calendar for 1973*, p. 119, in Russian.
** A. P. Timofievich, *We Were Guests at St. Seraphim's* (Jordanville, New York: Holy Trinity Monastery, 1953), in Russian.
*** One of these holy objects, an icon-portrait of St. Seraphim, is now in New Diveyevo Convent, Spring Valley, New York.

phim concerning the future of Russia. Further, we know from many indications that St. Seraphim himself is alive today in the hearts of many of the Russian people, even those who have been raised entirely under atheist influence. The following account, as recorded by S. Rozhdestvensky from the words of a Soviet Army officer who escaped to the West, is by no means a unique case of the presence of St. Seraphim in the suffering Russian land:

I was born and grew up in the city of Arzamas, near the former Sarov Monastery. If I am not mistaken, it was about 1929 when the Monastery with its very valuable and vast forest (a forest for building, as we say) was turned by the Soviet regime into a corrective labor camp. Not only the cells of the monks and the monastery buildings, but even the monastery churches (both summer and winter churches) were turned into barracks for prisoners. In the churches bunks were built in several layers, and the churches themselves were surrounded by barbed wire. But around the whole Monastery also rows of barbed wire extended, and there were watchtowers. What happened to the relics of St. Seraphim of Sarov I don't know. From my mother I heard that they were taken away somewhere, as they said, to one of the anti-religious museums of the land.

In these years when the corrective labor camp existed, narrow-gauge [railroad] lines were laid out throughout the Monastery in order to take out the trees. The forest was valuable and went, for the most part, for export abroad. In the neighborhood we often met parties of prisoners, with a guard of course, and sometimes with watchdogs also. In general it was not recommended for us free citizens to go near this concentration camp or express interest in it. In the end we also became used to it. And whenever echelons of prisoners would be unloaded at our stations, we young people would only shrug our shoulders. After all, these were enemies of the people, that's where they belonged.

I can add that before my very eyes the immensely valuable forest, in which bears had roamed, was greatly thinned; and of its previous grandeur we could judge only by the tales of my mother and acquaintances.

Once with a group of Pioneers (Communists "Scouts") I accidentally wandered across the mass graves of the prisoners, which were laid out near the

Monastery itself. Even then I was unpleasantly struck by the size of the cemetery. Dread overcame us Pioneers, and we quickly left. Later, in the long winter evenings, I sometimes listened in on mother's quiet conversation with some old women. They usually talked about the hundreds and thousands of prisoners who had been martyred by hunger and overwork. They sighed, oh-ed, and crossed themselves; and mother always wept because of these conversations. I knew that she was very religious and had hidden old icons somewhere, and that she went around to the churches which remained in Arzamas. She did not prevent me from living my own life: from the Pioneers I went to the Komsomol (Communist Youth), and then went away to study and work in a factory; and therefore I did not interfere in her private matters. But I did not ridicule her faith.

During the Second World War, I was sent from the army to military school. Before leaving for the front I was able to come home for a visit. This was in the summer of 1943. Mother once asked me to accompany her as far as the church. In that year two or three churches were opened in the city, it appears, and every prohibition against religion was lifted. Some kind of solemn service was going on in church. Mother even remarked to me that there they were going to pray for the granting of victory over the enemy and that now, in connection with the war, one could see many soldiers in the churches.

I went with mother, desiring to give her this small joy. Near the church, in fact, I noticed many paupers and likewise soldiers, who entered the church quite boldly. I also decided to look, and I entered with mother. We could hardly force ourselves into the church, there were so many people. In the middle of the church I noticed many candles in front of a large icon of Seraphim of Sarov, and even flowers around the icon-stand. The service was going on. But I did not stay in church long—I was unaccustomed to everything there, and to speak frankly, I was afraid that some one of my companions, former Komsomols, might see me there.

At night I left for the front. Just before my departure mother, of course, wept, and then somehow unexpectedly she told me: "I believe you will remain alive. I will pray, and he will preserve you!"

"Who is he?" I asked.

"Our saint, Seraphim of Sarov," mother answered.

Not desiring to offend mother, I answered her nothing then, but in my soul I only laughed at her prediction.

Oh yes, I should add that on this visit some icons were hanging openly in the corner of mother's room, and one of them was of St. Seraphim of Sarov. Mother explained to me that many people now had icons out. She related also that in the churches all the newly-born were being baptized, and boys were being given the name Seraphim. "In honor of our saint," she added.

At the front endless campaigns and battles began. I was slightly wounded twice, received decorations and promotions. Our regiment for its military merits was called a "guardian" regiment. At that time we all lived on the dream that the enemy would be quickly banished and destroyed.

In the summer of 1944, during the decisive battles on the Polish border, I was seriously wounded and lay unconscious for several days. As I found out later, the physicians had no hope that I would be saved. And then, believe it or not as you wish, at the moment when my body was fighting with death, I dreamed that I was again a Pioneer and that we were walking in the forest by Sarov Monastery—where we Pioneers had once come across the prisoners' cemetery. For some reason I became separated from the others. Some kind of terror overcame me. And suddenly an old man came out of the forest. He came up to me quickly, looked me right in the eyes, put his hand on my head, and said: "But you will live! Your mother obtained this by her prayers!..." And I had no time to come to myself or become afraid when he had already disappeared. I woke up.... I was in a hospital ward, not a forest. A doctor and a nurse were standing by my cot and saying something. I remember only one remark: "The crisis has passed!" I stubbornly tried to remember where I had met that old man before. Finally I remembered: in the church in Arzamas, on the icon. Then I gently fell asleep....

I lay in this hospital several weeks more and then again went to the front. I stormed the Oder, Berlin, climbed on German tanks, earned another two medals. One may say that I was in hell itself, but I was certain that I would remain alive. But why, actually, I was so certain—I could not explain to myself at that time....

The war ended. Our regiment remained in occupied Germany. At the end of 1947 I went home again. But I did not find my mother—she had died. I went to her grave in the city cemetery. On the way back from the cemetery, for some reason I decided to look at the church into which I had gone with my mother before leaving for the front. It was getting dark. In the half-lit church there were few people. I again saw that icon of Seraphim of Sarov. I looked at it, and something shuddered in my heart. I remembered my old mother. Coming out of the church, I turned my attention to the citizens who were hurrying along the streets. And I remarked to myself: in the victorious country everyone is dressed more poorly than the Germans. But more important: everyone's face looks worried, sad, and distressed....

Outside the church were invalids of the war, without legs, openly begging alms—yet another new blow and a new discovery. After looking all around, I inconspicuously gave them everything I had in my pocket. On the way to my friends', I noticed more of the same invalids. From my friends I found out that religion was again in disgrace and was being persecuted. Both icons and churches had again become dangerous things.

That evening I got drunk with my friends. Many of them were responsible workers, one of them, just like me, being a war hero. We recalled the Komsomol, the campaigns, the war. It's strange, but not a word was spoken about the future. I heard them talk, but I didn't understand them and only drank and drank. Concerning myself and my experiences I didn't say a single word to them. In the morning, before the end of my leave, I left my native Arzamas with the firm intention never to return.

At the station I accidentally came across a party of prisoners. They were being forced to walk under convoy to Sarov Monastery. And suddenly I caught myself in a traitorous thought: "You dogs! Before you at least unloaded the prisoners at night, but now you aren't ashamed to do it in the morning!"...

Well, later on, step by step everything began to be revealed to me anew. I began to see more often at night the little old man, Seraphim of Sarov. Now I understand that he was not like the rest of us.... And now you see, my eyes were opened so much that I escaped from there. And I do not regret it.*

---

* "Sarov Monastery," *New Russian Word,* August 1, 1970, in Russian.

This and numerous other testimonies give us no grounds to doubt that the great Saint Seraphim, even in bonds, is alive in Russia today and grants his aid as ever to the now-crucified Orthodox Russian people, who with him await in God's time, the day of deliverance.

Holy Father Seraphim, pray to God for us!

Monk Herman
Winter 1972

View of Diveyevo Convent. Lithograph, 1904.

APPENDIX II

Pascha in Summer

ST. SERAPHIM'S ARRIVAL AT DIVEYEVO

WITH the closure of the Sarov Monastery in early 1921, the monks were killed or driven away, and the relics of St. Seraphim were opened and examined by a Soviet government commission consisting of 157 men, which composed a detailed document based on its examination. In April of 1927 the relics were taken to Moscow and placed in an anti-religious museum. Due to their popular veneration, they were subsequently sent to the Kazan Cathedral in St. Petersburg (then known as Leningrad), which at that time was a "Museum of Religion and Atheism." There they remained hidden for over sixty years, until it pleased God to reveal them once again.

The two years leading up to 1988, the one-thousand-year anniversary of the baptism of Russia, were truly portentous for believers in Russia. During this period there was a tremendous leap in the number of believers. Government anti-religious policies were slightly relaxed. A great many churches, long closed or used for secular functions, were opened and renovated. Baptisms, of both adults and children, became commonplace. The death knell of the Communist state could be heard through the joyous ringing of newly re-hung church bells.

The next year, in the spring of 1989, the authorities began the return of the churches of the Diveyevo Convent to the Orthodox Church, starting with the wooden church dedicated to the Kazan Icon of the Theotokos. One year later the main cathedral, dedicated to the Holy Trinity, was reconsecrated. It was now time for St. Seraphim's return.

I.

THE SECOND UNCOVERING OF
THE RELICS OF ST. SERAPHIM

In December of 1990, the decision was made to remove the museum of religion and atheism from the Kazan Cathedral in St. Petersburg. In one of the storage vaults which contained tapestries, a large bast mat was found. When this mat was unfolded, the relics of a saint were discovered inside. These relics could not be identified according to the inventory lists of the atheist museum. The relics wore a copper cross, and gloves were on the hands. On one glove was embroidered "Holy Father Seraphim," and on the other, "Pray to God for Us."

A Church commission was formed and, making use of the document that had been compiled at the opening of the saint's relics in 1921, the members came to the indisputable conclusion that these were in fact the relics of St. Seraphim. Reports about the second uncovering of the holy relics of St. Seraphim the Wonderworker of Sarov began to spread throughout St. Petersburg by the end of December. The official confirmation came on the day of Christ's Nativity, December 25, 1990/January 7, 1991, when Metropolitan John of St. Petersburg and Ladoga, after completing the Divine Liturgy, proclaimed to the clergy and laity that the holy relics of the saint had indeed been found again. On December 29/January 11 the relics were officially given to the Church by the museum and were then brought to the St. Alexander Nevsky Lavra for public veneration.

The relics remained in St. Petersburg until the feast day of St. Xenia, January 24/February 6, when they were placed in a special railroad car and brought to Moscow. There they were triumphantly met by believers and taken to the Holy Theophany Patriarchal Cathedral in an enormous proces-

Procession with the relics of St. Seraphim through the streets of Moscow in 1991.

sion. More than twenty bishops were present there to serve a Moleben of Thanksgiving. The relics of the God-pleaser remained in the Theophany Cathedral to be venerated by the large crowds that gathered there daily from all corners of Russia, as well as from abroad. Molebens were served continually, as well as the Akathist to the saint:

> *Rejoice, thou who art glorified by the Lord through a multitude of miracles;*
> *Rejoice, thou who hast shone forth to the whole world by thy love;*
> *Rejoice, boast and joy of the holy Church;*
> *Rejoice, glory and defense of the Russian realm.*
> *Rejoice, O venerable Father Seraphim, wonderworker of Sarov!*

On July 10/23—to the ringing of bells and accompanied by the Patriarch, numerous bishops and clergy, and many thousands of believers—the saint's relics were carried in a week-long procession to Diveyevo, which only a

Present-day panoramic view of Diveyevo Convent from the southwest.

Diveyevo's Holy Trinity Cathedral, the resting place of St. Seraphim's relics.

week earlier had been officially re-opened as a convent by decree of the Holy Synod. The procession made its way through the countryside, passing through several cities and towns, such as Bogorodsk, Vladimir, Nizhni Novgorod, and Arzamas, and stopping at numerous churches along the way for the serving of All-night Vigils, as well as Molebens to the saint. The Patriarch of Moscow and All Russia, Alexei II, accompanied the relics over the entire course of the procession. At one point during the procession he said: "We are living through a complex time. It is a time of confrontations, contradictions, and intolerance. It is at this time that the second uncovering of the relics of St. Seraphim of Sarov is taking place. And again, with enormous power, his instruction comes to life: 'Acquire the spirit of peace and thousands around you will be saved.' St. Seraphim, who taught for so long and so meekly about the acquisition of the Holy Spirit, reminds us all once again today about the peaceful Christian spirit. The urgency of this call is obvious. One wants to cry out to the saint in a heartfelt, prayerful appeal: 'O our Father Seraphim! During thy life thou wast a source of Divine love and joy. Now, as we stand before the reliquary containing thy holy relics, we beseech thee: teach us fraternal love and joy in the Holy Spirit; help us to overcome all disagreements and confusion; grant peace and prosperity to the Holy Church and to our fatherland, on this day and in the times to come.'"

At last, on the evening of July 17/30, 1991, two days short of the eighty-eighth anniversary of the glorification of St. Seraphim, the saint's relics arrived at Diveyevo, the convent that he had founded and directed. The crowds that greeted them there were enormous, reminding one of Abbess Maria's prophecy in 1903.*

Several remarkable events took place at the time of the arrival of the relics at Diveyevo. Before St. Seraphim's repose he had given a candle to Praskovia Semyonovna Meliukova, the sister of St. Martha of Diveyevo, saying that the sisters would meet him in Diveyevo with that candle. It was carefully preserved for almost 160 years until that July day in 1991. The last guardian of the candle was Schemanun Margarita (Lakhtionova), the only surviving nun who had lived in the convent before it was closed. This candle was mounted in a larger candle and held by the serving deacon at the first Moleben served before the holy relics at their arrival. Additionally, a small amount of incense, likewise

---

* See p. 126.

The reliquary of St. Seraphim
as it looks today.

handed down from the saint, was used. At the time of the service, two of the convent sisters, who were at their obedience selling books at a booth and were thus saddened at being unable to be present in the church, were consoled by seeing the sun dance and shine with all the colors of the rainbow. At another place some pilgrims saw what appeared to be a pillar of light by the cathedral church.

On July 18/31, the eve of the saint's summer feast, the relics were brought into the center of the church and a festal All-night Vigil was served. At midnight, the first of four Liturgies was served. Instead of the usual Communion hymns, the sisters began to sing the irmosi of the Paschal Canon, and all the people present joined them. The fourth Liturgy, served by Patriarch Alexei, took place outdoors, at the large square in front of the Holy Trinity Cathedral. Patriarch Alexei said at the time: "We have seen with what spiritual joy the precious holy treasure of our Church—the holy relics of the venerable one—has been met everywhere. Our hearts have been filled with true Paschal joy, and we have sung the Paschal hymns, recalling his words, that Pascha would be sung in the middle of summer. A new page begins in the history of the Diveyevo Convent."

Many of the holy objects associated with St. Seraphim, long safeguarded by nuns and pious lay folk from the hands of the Communists, have been returned and now reside in Diveyevo. Among them are the icon of the Most Holy Theotokos, "Joy of All Joys," before which the saint reposed, his cauldron in which he used to store dried bread for distribution to pilgrims as blessings, and various articles of his clothing.

The events attending on the discovery and transfer of St. Seraphim's relics to Diveyevo contributed to a much-needed movement of repentance throughout Russia. The Russian people began a process of national catharsis to help them wash off the fetor of almost seventy-five years of Communist domination. This movement was not without results—almost exactly a year after the discovery of the relics of St. Seraphim, the Communist government was officially dissolved on December 13/26, 1991. A culminating moment in this movement occurred on August 7/20, 2000, when the

Recent photograph of St. Seraphim's *kanavka* (at right), and the path used by those reciting his prayer rule.

Russian Orthodox Church glorified the New Martyrs and Confessors of Russia in the newly rebuilt and reconsecrated Cathedral of Christ the Savior in Moscow.

Since the translation of St. Seraphim's relics to Diveyevo, all of Diveyevo's churches have been remodeled, and the entire convent now sparkles with beauty. One important feature that has been restored is St. Seraphim's *kanavka*.* Not long before his repose, the saint told the sisters at Diveyevo to dig a trench around the monastery property. He told them that the Mother of God herself would walk around that path, and he gave the sisters a prayer rule to perform as they walked around it daily: to repeat "O

---

* *Kanavka:* a trench or canal.

Theotokos and Virgin, rejoice…" one hundred fifty times, saying "Our Father…" after every tenth repetition. Here are some quotes about the *kanavka* attributed to St. Seraphim:

"It is necessary to dig a *kanavka,* three yards deep and three yards wide, so that thieves will not get across."

"I'm telling you, Matushka, what joy we'll have there! We'll have our own land, and we'll dig a *kanavka* around the convent. And when we dig it, visitors will come to us and will take clay from it for healing, and for them it will ttake the place of gold!"

"This *kanavka* is in the footsteps of the Mother of God. The Queen of Heaven herself has walked around it, and has taken the convent as her portion. This *kanavka* is as high as heaven! When Antichrist comes, he will get in everywhere, but he won't be able to jump across this *kanavka!…* He who walks around the *kanavka* with prayer and repeats 'O Theotokos and Virgin Rejoice' 150 times, for him this place will be Athos, Jerusalem and Kiev!"

"When time is coming to an end, the Antichrist will begin to take down crosses from churches and monasteries, and will destroy all the monasteries. And he'll come up to your monastery, he'll come up to it, but the *kanavka* will rise from earth to heaven, and he won't be able to get in. The *kanavka* won't let him get in anywhere, and so he'll go away."

During the Communist persecutions the *kanavka* was filled in and various outbuildings were built across the path. Beginning in 2003, as the convent regained control of the land, the *kanavka* was redug, and a flagstone path was laid beside it for the nuns and their pilgrims to walk as they continue to recite St. Seraphim's prayer rule.

2.

NEW GLORIFICATIONS

On September 13/26, 2000, the incorrupt relics of Nun Elena (Manturova) were uncovered next to the church dedicated to the Kazan Icon of the Theotokos. On the following day the relics of Abbess Alexandra (Melgunova), the foundress and first abbess of Diveyevo, and Schemanun

Martha (Meliukova) were also uncovered. They were brought into the Church of the Nativity of the Theotokos, where St. Seraphim had prophesied that they would repose. Later that year, on December 9/22, the anniversary of the founding of the Mill Convent for virgins, located within the boundaries of the Diveyevo Convent, these three God-pleasers were glorified as locally venerated saints of the Nizhni Novgorod diocese.

Beginning in 2001, several New Martyrs of Diveyevo were entered into the list of saints: Hieromartyr Michael (Gusev), Nun-martyr Pelagia (Testova), and Nun-confessor Matrona (Vlasova). The following year Nun-martyr Martha (Testova) was added, and in 2003 Hieromartyr James (Gusev).

Finally, in January of 2004, the relics of three Fools-for-Christ's-sake who labored in Diveyevo were uncovered and brought to the convent's Kazan Church for veneration. These were Blessed Pelagia (Serebrennikova), who reposed in 1884; Schemanun Parasceva (also known as Pasha of Sarov), who reposed in 1915; and Blessed Maria (Fedina), who reposed in 1931. They were glorified at Diveyevo as locally venerated saints on July 19/August 1, 2004, in connection with the celebration of the 250th anniversary of the birth of St. Seraphim. On September 23/October 6 of the same year, the Holy Synod of the Russian Orthodox Church approved their Church-wide glorification.

3.

SAROV MONASTERY

Upon the forced closure of Sarov Monastery in 1927, the monastery was used for three years as a work commune for homeless children, who had been gathered from all over the country. Beginning in 1931, the area was used by the NKVD* as a corrective labor camp for adolescents and adults, and during this time a woodworking factory was built there. This lasted until 1938. During the Second World War more factories were built at Sarov, this time for the production of weapons. As men were sent to the front, their places in the factories were taken by women. In 1946, the area in which Sarov

---

* NKVD: The state security department, which later became the KGB.

Monastery was located (by then a city) was named Arzamas-16, and it was here that the Soviets developed their first atomic bomb. The city was designated as a restricted area, and entrance to outsiders was forbidden.

Finally, in 1989, after sixty-two years without a single church service in Sarov, Archbishop Nicholas of Arzamas served a Moleben at the site of St. Seraphim's Far Hermitage. At the begining of 1990 the first parish in the city was formed, composed of scientists and workers from the restricted city. In the summer of 1991, in connection with the procession of the relics of St. Seraphim to Diveyevo, the parish was allowed to be officially registered. On the day after the arrival of the saint's relics at Diveyevo, Patriarch Alexei visited Sarov for the first time and led a procession, accompanied by several thousand local people, from the city to the site of St. Seraphim's Far Hermitage, where he blessed a cross and a memorial statue of the saint.

In 1992 the first priest, a former scientist, arrived in the city, which had by then reverted to its original name of Sarov. In the beginning, services were celebrated in a newly built chapel at the city cemetery, but on the day of Pentecost the Federal Nuclear Center gave the monastery church of All saints (which had been used as a store) to the parish. The first service was celebrated there on the feast of the Protection of the Most Holy Theotokos. At about the same time a Sunday school and a series of courses for adults on the Orthodox Faith were organized at the parish. The following year an additional priest was assigned to the parish, and in 1995 a third priest. In 1996, there began an annual procession from Sarov to Diveyevo and back, taking place on the summer feast of St. Seraphim. In 1999 the Nuclear Center gave another monastery church back to the Orthodox Church: that of St. John the Forerunner, which had been used as an administrative building. This church was remodeled and reconsecrated in 2000. In 2003, the Church of St. Seraphim, built a hundred years earlier on the occasion of the saint's glorification, was re-consecrated by Patriarch Alexei (see below).

By 2006 there were seven open churches in Sarov. That year the Sarov Monastery, by decision of the Holy Synod, was reopened, and three monks were blessed to take up residence there. The superior is Hieromonk Barnabas (Baranov). Due to security concerns, Sarov remains a closed city, closed even to pilgrims, and this will be the case for the foreseeable future.

Patriarch Alexei, standing before the relics of St. Seraphim,
addresses believers in Sarov. Standing in front of the other microphone
is Russian President Vladimir Putin. July 17/30, 2003.

4.

RECENT EVENTS

The summer feast day of St. Seraphim in 2003 marked the hundredth
anniversary of his glorification. To celebrate this event, four days of festivities
were scheduled. Beginning on July 16/29, there was a festal Liturgy served by
Patriarch Alexei at Diveyevo, attended by huge crowds of people. After the
Liturgy, there was a triumphant procession with the saint's relics to Sarov, a
distance of twelve miles. About twenty thousand people took part in the procession, which lasted over five hours. That evening an All-night Vigil was celebrated at the newly and beautifully remodeled Sarov Monastery Church of

St. Seraphim. The next morning Patriarch Alexei performed the consecration of the church, followed by the Divine Liturgy. Among the concelebrants were Patriarch Pavle of the Serbian Orthodox Church, representatives of the Patriarchates of Jerusalem, Constantinople, Antioch, Alexandria, Georgia, Romania, and Bulgaria, representatives of the Churches of Ukraine, Belarus, Estonia, Poland, Cyprus, Greece, Albania, the Czech lands, Slovakia, Japan, and America, and almost all the diocesan bishops of the Russian Orthodox Church.

The following morning there was a Moleben, attended by Russian President Vladimir Putin, who had given a four-and-a-half-ton bell to the Sarov Monastery. He also gave an icon of St. Seraphim to the Patriarch, which the latter gave to the Diveyevo Convent. Patriarch Alexei noted that, because Tsar Nicholas II, the head of the Russian government, took part in the glorification of St. Seraphim one hundred years earlier, it was fitting that the present head of the Russian government take part in that day's celebration. After the Moleben St. Seraphim's relics were taken in procession back to Diveyevo. The next morning, on the birthday of the saint and the hundredth anniversary of his glorification, Patriarch Alexei celebrated the Divine Liturgy with all of his previous concelebrants at an altar in the square before the Holy Trinity Cathedral in Diveyevo. The twenty thousand believers present felt the Paschal joy of the event, and the Patriarch often turned to them during the service to cry out, "Christ is risen!" The exclamations at the Liturgy were given in the languages of the Local Orthodox Churches. To commune the faithful it was necessary to use fifty chalices. Many of the participants, in keeping with Russian tradition, came to the celebrations on foot. According to Abbess Sergia of Diveyevo, at least ten different processions came from places like Moscow, Sergiev Posad, Sochi, Ekaterinburg, and even Siberia.

The year 2004 marked the 250th anniversary of the birth of St. Seraphim.* To mark the occasion, the saint's relics were brought in procession on July 7/20 to Kursk, his home city, where they remained for three days. The officiating hierarch was Metropolitan Vladimir of Kiev, the Exarch of the

---

* Thanks to extensive research by historian Valentin Alexandrovich Stepashkin, it has been determined that the year of St. Seraphim's birth was actually 1754, and not 1759, as was previously believed.

Left: The newly remodeled Church of St. Seraphim at Sarov Monastery.

Below: Hierarchs from many Local Orthodox Churches serving at the consecration of the St. Seraphim Church in July 2003.

Ukraine, who was joined by more than fifty other hierarchs from Russia, the Ukraine, and Belarus. During this time in Kursk the saint's relics were brought to the site where the house once stood in which the saint was born, and where there now stands a chapel, which was consecrated at this time. During their stay in Kursk the holy relics were placed in the cathedral church of the Monastery of the Sign, where up to 150,000 believers venerated them. On July 10/23, after the celebration of the Divine Liturgy and a Moleben, the relics were briefly brought to St. Sergius-Kazan Icon Cathedral, which was built by St. Seraphim's parents. Beside the cathedral is a monument which marks the spot where young Prochor Moshnin, the future St. Seraphim, fell from the top of the cathedral when it was under construction. The relics were then returned to Diveyevo.

The main celebrations in Diveyevo began on July 18/31, and were led by Metropolitan Philaret of Minsk, the Exarch of Belarus, assisted by many other bishops. On that day he consecrated the newly remodeled Church of the Kazan Icon of the Theotokos. It was on the site of this church that the Mother of God herself appeared to St. Alexandra, the foundress and first abbess of Diveyevo, and directed her to build the church. On July 19/August 1, after the first Liturgy in this church, which was attended by over five thousand pilgrims, Metropolitan Philaret performed the glorification of the three Fools-for-Christ's-Sake of Diveyevo: Pelagia, Pasha of Sarov, and Maria. Later that day Metropolitan Kirill of Smolensk consecrated a new middle school in the town of Diveyevo.

At the present time Diveyevo Convent is one of the most popular pilgrimage sites in Russia. There are over four hundred nuns living there under the guidance of Abbess Sergia. The town of Diveyevo has become an international pilgimage center, and the whole region is regularly filled with those desiring to pray before St. Seraphim's relics, to beseech him for healing of soul and body. Truly the saint's prophecy is coming true: that he "would go from Sarov to Diveyevo," that "a great multitude of people will assemble from all the ends of the earth," and that "Diveyevo will become a lavra."

St. Herman of Alaska Brotherhood
Great Lent, 2008

INDEX

soul,
  care for, 40–41
  nourishment of, 41–42
  peace of, 42–43
Spyridon of Tremithus, St., 45
Stepashkin, Valentin Alexandrovich, 152 n.
Stephen the New, St., 59
superiors, duties of those subject to, 39
sybils, virgin-prophetesses, 92
Symeon the God-receiver, St., 26, 92
Symeon the New Theologian, St., 30

tears, 30–31
temptations, vigilance against, 54
Theodore the Studite, St., 9
Theodosius the Younger, Emperor, 121–23, 125

Theognostus, St., 110, 123 n.
Theophan of Poltava, Archbishop, 9–10
Theophan the Recluse, St., 7–8
Theophany Cathedral, Moscow, 142–43
Tikhon of Zadonsk, St., 7
Trinity, Holy, 24
truths, the keeping of recognized, 27–28

Urusova, Natalia Vladimirovna, Countess, 128–29

Valaam Elders, 10
Valaam Monastery, 8, 145, 148–49
Veronica, Nun, 133
Vladimir, Metropolitan of Kiev, 152–53
Vitaly, Archbishop of Jordanville, 9–10

ST. HERMAN OF ALASKA BROTHERHOOD

For over four decades, the St. Herman Brotherhood has been publishing
works of traditional Orthodox Christianity.
Write for our free catalogue, featuring over fifty titles.

St. Herman Press
P. O. Box 70
Platina, CA 96076

Visit our website and order online from:
www.sainthermanpress.com